WADSWORTH PH*

GW01044190

ON

RICOEUR

Mark Muldoon
Brock University

Australia • Canada • Mexico • Singapore • Spain
United Kingdom • United States

Printed in the United States of America
1 2 3 4 5 6 7 05 04 03 02 01

For permission to use material from this text, contact us:
Web: http://www.thomsonrights.com
Fax: 1-800-730-2215
Phone: 1-800-730-2214

For more information, contact:
Wadsworth/Thomson Learning, Inc.
10 Davis Drive
Belmont, CA 94002-3098
USA
http://www.wadsworth.com

ISBN: 0-534-58399-7

Contents

Preface

Chapter 1: The Philosopher and His Tasks................1
    Introduction 1
    Life and Major Works..6
    Perspectives 12
    Influences...14

Chapter 2: The Early Works.............................20
    Freedom and Nature..20
    Fallibility...24
    The Symbolism of Evil 31

Chapter 3: From Symbol to Text.....................36
    Freud 37
    Language as Discourse....................................45
    World of the Text 50
    Texts and Hermeneutics..................................53

Chapter 4: Imagination: Metaphor and Narrative...........57
    Metaphor..58
    Narrative and Time..63
    Narrative Identity 74
    Ideology and Utopia..78

Chapter 5: The Self, the Other and Justice 83
    The Primacy of Ethics over Morality 83
    Moral Agency and the Other............................87
    Justice..91
    Practical Wisdom 93

Preface

At the dawn of the new millennium Paul Ricoeur (b. 1913) is recognized as one of the most influential of living French philosophers. His influence extends beyond philosophy and includes significant contributions to the human sciences, literary criticism, historiography, interpretation theory, politics, ethics and theology. Ricoeur is acknowledged primarily for his efforts in bringing together many of the important themes of 20th century philosophy and showing how language – especially that which is poetic and metaphoric – becomes the chosen place to construct meaning and to understand existence through interpretation.

Along with Heidegger and Gadamer, Ricoeur is a central figure in pushing German phenomenology beyond the limits of its eidetic method in order to give it a particular hermeneutical orientation. The point of this hermeneutical turn was not to further the project of description at either the transcendental or existential level but to reveal how any description is already an interpretation. One underlying assumption behind a phenomenological hermeneutics is that consciousness is not universal or transcendental in structure but must be approached through its objectification in cultural artifacts that include documents, actions, texts, monuments and institutions. As a consequence, what we can know about our human existence, and the capacities of our being, can only be studied indirectly by interpreting what has been deposited in the past at different times and in different cultures.

Ricoeur's project however does not limit itself to merely uncovering meaning or showing how meaning is mediated by symbols, myths and language. Integral to elaborating what he calls a philosophical anthropology, Ricoeur is specifically interested in revealing how the interplay of the productive imagination and language facilitates the creation of meaning by way of metaphor and narrative. In uncovering the nature of the narrative function, Ricoeur wishes to show how the construction of plots provides a "readability" to our experience and how the "world of the text" offers the reader novel opportunities for thinking and acting differently. Human reflection is thus highly dependent on works and signs the interpretation of which does not culminate in knowledge for knowledge sake but in the self-knowledge of the subject who understands him or herself better. The importance of such an analysis becomes all the more evident in Ricoeur's later works where he discusses the ethical capacities of the human subject as the intersection between identity, institutions and practical wisdom.

On Ricoeur is written with new readers to Ricoeur in mind. It limits its scope to surveying Ricoeur's philosophical works to the exclusion of his numerous other writings that address both theological and political issues. Each of Ricoeur's major works is an expression of a method and analysis that is not summarized in any one of his books. Ricoeur's writings truly reflect a philosopher whose thought is always in progress and on the way. Owing to his particular style of rigorous engagement with a wide variety of thinkers, an attempt has been made to present Ricoeur's thought in the wake of these engagements in order to present a type of blueprint of his own original contributions to philosophical thinking. Wherever possible, references have been given not only to passages in his major works but also to his collections of essays that clarify and augment his central theses. The hope behind *On Ricoeur* is that it acts as an invitation for students and scholars to turn to the major works themselves in order to experience their richness and vitality.

Abbreviations of Cited Works

All publication dates for books cited in the text refer to the year the book originally appeared, most likely in French. For complete bibliographic details, readers are referred to the current bibliography (2000) cited in the first endnote of Chapter One. A more concise bibliography (1995) is found in PR.

CC	*Critique and Conviction* (1995)
CI	*Conflict of Interpretations: Essays in Hermeneutics* (1969)
FM	*Fallible Man (1960)*
FN	*Freedom and Nature: The Voluntary and the Involuntary* (1950)
FP	*Freud and Philosophy: An Essay on Interpretation* (1965)
FT	*From Text to Action: Essays in Hermeneutics, II* (1986)
HS	*Hermeneutics and the Human Sciences* (1981)
HA	*Husserl: An Analysis of his Phenomenology* (1967)
HT	*History and Truth* (1955)
IT	*Interpretation Theory* (1976)
IU	*Lectures on Ideology and Utopia* (1986)
OA	*Oneself as Another* (1990)
PA	*The Philosophy of Paul Ricoeur: An Anthology of his Works* (1978)
PR	*The Philosophy of Paul Ricoeur* (ed. Lewis Edwin Hahn) (1995)
RI	*A Ricoeur Reader: Imagination and Reflection* (1986)
RM	*The Rule of Metaphor* (1975)
SE	*The Symbolism of Evil* (1960)
TJ	*The Just* (1995)
TN	*Time and Narrative* (3 vols.) (1983-5)

1
The Philosopher and His Tasks

Introduction

A recent bibliography attributes more than a dozen major works to the name of Paul Ricoeur, including several texts of collected essays and almost 700 professional articles.[1] What is immediately apparent from even a cursory review of these works is the restless and dynamic nature of their topics and analysis. Beginning with his personal assimilation of Husserlian phenomenology, Ricoeur moves toward a hermeneutical method with which he will make continual incursions into almost every tradition in Western philosophy. Given the breadth of his interests, Ricoeur's thinking does not lend itself to a tidy description. Famous for his rich engagements with such diverse fields as psychoanalysis, structuralism, action theory and the narrative function, Ricoeur readily admits to "a certain lack of continuity" in his writings. He sees himself responding to challenges rather than adding to the development of a unique project. While he consistently refers to his works as a contribution toward a "philosophical anthropology," his program for presenting such an anthropology is not easily summarized. None of Ricoeur's major works represents a final consolidation. Furthermore, many new readers often note the tentativeness of his conclusions and the endless multiplication of problems issuing from his starting points.

There are two reasons that account for this discontinuity and tentativeness. First, Ricoeur subjects his thinking to a regulative ideal that purposely denies the possibility of a final synthesis. While never abandoning the tradition of rationality first characterized by the Greeks (CI 296), Ricoeur defines reason in its broadest sense as the persistent quest for unity (HT 165ff). Such a unity however must make a fragile passage between two temptations: one that wishes to forge a final and immediate synthesis of truth and one that encourages the multiplication of conflicting philosophies. The danger of synthesis lies in the mere presumption of unity and a possible dogmatism that often leads to the violent misuse of the synthesis. On the other hand, the constant fragmentation of philosophies easily leads to skepticism and thereby abandons the hope for unity. To avoid such temptations, Ricoeur sees himself working under the aegis of what he calls a limit concept. Borrowed from Kant, this means that the unity of truth is seen as an ideal that can never be known in itself. Its role is to limit those sorts of claims to a final synthesis that one might be tempted to make in the course of a philosophical analysis. For Ricoeur:

> The last word therefore is not uttered anywhere; I do not yet know how to Say it and Make it consistent with everything else: how, for example, perceptual truth, scientific truth, ethical truth, etc., coincide. I do not know how Plato, Aristotle, Descartes, Kant, and Hegel share in the same truth (HT 12).

While invoked to preserve philosophic hope and to avoid any claims to absolute knowledge, the application of such a limit concept turns the unity of truth into a timeless task. Rationality remains a continual project rather than a possession. Even at the risk of seeming tentative and inconclusive, therefore, each of Ricoeur's works represents a renewed effort and a fresh movement of thought *in hope* of a synthesis that is not permitted to succumb to the Hegelian temptation of a final unity.[2]

There is perhaps a more decisive reason that explains the seemingly indefinite nature of Ricoeur's philosophical works and their trajectory. Ricoeur's philosophical method is often referred to as a "phenomenological hermeneutics." In very general terms phenomenology can be defined as the science of human experience and hermeneutics has often been summarized as the science of interpretation. Ricoeur "grafts" both terms together to denote a certain approach to human existence and its interrogation. The aim of the method is to make explicit the meaning of human existence or, more specifically, to elucidate what it means to be an acting human subject. The method assumes the primacy of the prephilosophical nature of our experience and the submission of that experience to a back and forth movement between an analytical-style explanation and an understanding open to interpretation.

Phenomenological hermeneutics as a philosophical method is the product of a fundamental assumption on the part of Ricoeur, namely, that knowledge of our existence and our own identities is a task to be achieved. Knowledge of human existence does not originate in consciousness. Such understanding can only be reached through an encounter with representations, actions, texts, institutions and monuments that objectify existence and mediate it. This is why Ricoeur describes the rhythm of his "philosophical respiration as one of detour and return."[3] The task of the philosopher is to pass through these objectifications of human existence and by means of analysis and interpretation return with a more productive understanding of the possible levels of meaning embodied in them.

In terms of human identity, for example, Ricoeur rejects the very possibility of a human being knowing him or herself immediately without *reflection*. He denies "the claim of immediacy, adequation, and apodicity made by the Cartesian cogito and the Kantian 'I think'" (PR 4). Human identity is not a pure act of self-transparency or the result of a direct intuition. Ricoeur's famous formula is that there is "no self-understanding that is not *mediated* by signs, symbols, and texts" (FT 15). This means that the individual subject cannot grasp his or her own act of existing except by interpreting the signs scattered in an external world not of his or her own making. Each of us is placed in a language that exists outside of ourselves before we possess our individual selves in consciousness. And even here the possession is never complete. We recover the self through constant interpretation.

Consequently, phenomenological hermeneutics is a "second-order" elucidation of a nebula of meaning that is already there in a prephilosophical manner. It is this nebula of meaning already there in a precomprehensible way that lends itself to thinking. In a celebrated passage Ricoeur coined a maxim that characterizes his general hermeneutics:

> 'Symbol gives rise to thought.' This maxim that I find so appealing says two things. The symbol gives: I do not posit the meaning, the symbol gives it; but what it gives is something for thought, something to think about. First the giving, then the positing; the phrase suggests, therefore, both that everything has already been said in enigma and yet that it is necessary ever to begin again and rebegin everything in the dimension of thought (CI 288).

3

Ricoeur's works are about beginnings and re-beginnings in attempt to recuperate in thought what is already given not only in symbols but in myths, actions and narratives of all sorts. The key problem of retrieving thought through various objectifications of human existence is the overdetermination of meaning. In the absence of absolute truths and transcendental standpoints interpretation gives rise to "double meanings," "multiple meanings" and eventually a "surplus of meaning." One of Ricoeur's oft-quoted statements is that in existence there is a "super-abundance of meaning to the abundance of non-sense" (CI 411). The result is an inevitable "conflict of interpretations" (HS 193). Such conflict is an inescapable consequence of the philosopher's decision to hold a final synthesis in abeyance and permit the hermeneutic detour the widest possible latitude.

Ricoeur's writing style is emblematic of this conflict. He rarely criticizes other positions and constantly notes his indebtedness to other authors. More to the point, Ricoeur is famous for purposely cultivating numerous dialectical and aporetic conflicts where seemingly irreconcilable oppositions are brought into sharp contrast. The point of encouraging such conflicts is to mediate differences – while preserving them – and to discover unrecognized connections. While arguably ponderous, such mediations are an impressive feature in opening dialogues between, for example, writing history and writing fiction, or, between Anglo-Saxon and Continental philosophy.

Scholars and students have been receptive to Ricoeur's ideas for many reasons but perhaps one is important to mention in the beginning. Given his profound focus on the human condition and its constraints, Ricoeur never gives in to a dour pessimism about existence. Where Jean-Paul Sartre (1905-1980) argued for the absence of meaning in existence and saw dread and anxiety as the basic human effect, Ricoeur will describe his philosophy as "a style of 'yes' and not a style of 'no,' and perhaps even a style characterized by joy and not by anguish" (HT 305). For Ricoeur joy has an equal claim to being an ontological effect over against feelings of alienation.

Such optimism is not grounded in an idealistic metaphysics or a masked theology. It is derived from a metaphysical category – or "metacategory" – that governs Ricoeur's philosophical anthropology, namely, being as act and potentiality (HT 328; OA 303ff). Simply put, to exist is to act. The very "being" of human beings is to act and the effort to be. Traditionally, "being" has been considered under the category of substance. This reduces "being" to a mere representation or idea. If being is nothing more than a brute datum, substance or a dead

4

thing, then the place of freedom becomes questionable if not impossible. The effort to exist, Ricoeur contends, is an originating affirmation both fundamental and primordial to human beings (HT 288). This affirmation is not necessarily self-evident or *a priori*. Before his hermeneutical turn in the early 1960s, Ricoeur suggested that some sense of this originating affirmation could be recovered or restored by experiences of negation. In every negative experience of our finite existence – which includes indignation, doubt, failure, recrimination, and anguish – there is a movement that transgresses this finitude. Too often this movement – this intense passion for existence – becomes obscured by overvaluing negativity as it has been in the case of Sartre. But the passion to exist is more primary than the failure and dread of existence. "Under the pressure of the negative, of negative experiences, we must re-achieve a notion of being which is *act* rather than *form*, living affirmation, the power of existing and of making exist" (HT 328). In the very least, regardless of the burden of our finitude and the weight of negation, we feel at the core of our being the effort to be. But "since our power to be has been alienated ... this effort remains a desire, the desire to be." It is a desire that affirms being within the lack of being (CI 452). For this reason human existence is forward oriented. It projects itself in front of itself towards possible ways of being. Seen under the sign of affirmation existence becomes the "passion for the possible" (CI 411). Primary affirmation is "secretly armed with hope" (HT 304).

Later, when Ricoeur turned to study the narrative function across multiple modes, he articulated this sense of affirmation in a different manner. The entire thrust of hermeneutics is to bring to light the ability of the poetic uses of language to provoke us – the readers – to live and to act differently. He argues that discourse never exists for its own sake, for its own glory, but that in all of its uses it seeks to bring into language an experience, a way of living in and of Being-in-the-world which precedes it and which demands to be said. He is passionately insistent on preventing language from closing up on itself and forfeiting its power to pursue such a reference.

> It is this conviction that there is always a *Being-demanding to be said* (*un être-à-dire*) that precedes our actual saying which explains my obstinacy in trying to discover in the poetic uses of language the referential mode appropriate to them through which discourse continues to 'say' Being even when it appears to have withdrawn into itself for the sake of self-celebration (FT 19).

5

Life and Major Works

Paul Ricoeur has lived an extraordinary life.[4] Born in Valence in 1913, his mother died shortly after his birth. Two years later his father would be killed in the Battle of the Marne. Raised in the devout Protestant household of his paternal grandparents at Rennes, Ricoeur carried the label of being an "orphan of the state" from his earliest school days until his graduation from university. After completing his *Licence-ès-lettres* from the University of Rennes in 1933, Ricoeur enrolled the following year at the Sorbonne in Paris. Over the next several years he would start a family and teach in two different lycées before his young professional life was radically interrupted with the outbreak of the Second World War.

In 1939, while studying German in Munich, Ricoeur was recalled to France and mobilized into the army. Decorated for his valor in combat, Ricoeur was eventually captured by the enemy and he remained a prisoner-of-war until liberation in 1945. Regardless of the atmosphere of the prison camp Ricoeur found himself in the company of stimulating French intellectuals like Mikel Dufrenne (1910-1995) and Roger Ikor (1912-1986). Once organized, this group provided the structure for serious philosophical reading, discussions and teaching. During this time Ricoeur not only wrote the outlines and initials drafts of his first works but, writing minutely in the margins of the book, he completed his translation of Edmund Husserl's (1859-1938) *Ideas I*.

Shortly after the war the fruits of his long detainment began to show itself. In 1947, Ricoeur published a co-authored work with Mikel Dufrenne on the philosophy of Karl Jaspers (*Karl Jaspers et la philosophie de l'existence*). In the following year, Ricoeur released a work comparing the two philosophies of Gabriel Marcel and Jaspers (*Gabriel Marcel et Karl Jaspers: Philosophie du mystère et philosophie du paradoxe*). Both works are expository in nature and today remain untranslated into English. It was his French translation of Husserl's work, published later as the minor thesis for his doctorate that would establish Ricoeur as one of the leading phenomenological scholars of the day.

Owing to the fact that war affected both his childhood and his adult life it is not unlikely that the questions of politics and ethics would find a central place in Ricoeur's overall philosophical anthropology of the acting and suffering human subject. Prior to the Second World War most of his published articles dealt with the topics of Christian socialism and pacifism. While such concerns certainly reflect his contacts with personalities as Emmanuel Mounier (1905-1950) and the socialist André Philip (1902-1970) their roots go much deeper. As a young child Ricoeur learned of the injustice resulting from the Treaty of Versailles. It necessitated the serious re-consideration of his father's death on the battlefield. "Stripped of any reassuring halo of a just war and of a stainless victory, his death proved to be a death for nothing" (PR 8). Such sentiments made pacifism an obvious choice. Over the course of his life Ricoeur has maintained a strong belief in pacifism often through association with various communities inspired by the spirit of Quakerism. Despite such sympathies he readily admits that Nazism taught him that absolute pacifism might not be the appropriate response in all cases (CC 16).

Immediately following the war Ricoeur taught for two years in the south of France, at Collège Cévenol in Chambon-sur-Lignon. In 1948, he was called to succeed Jean Hyppolite (1907-1968) in the history of philosophy at the University of Strasbourg. Two years later *Freedom and Nature: The Voluntary and the Involuntary* appeared fulfilling the requirements for Ricoeur's *Doctorat-ès-lettres*. The work constituted the first volume of a projected three-volume study whose overall title would be *Philosophy of the Will*. This early work is a modified phenomenological analysis of the human will intertwined with existential themes. The thesis asserts that human freedom is not absolute but tempered between what we voluntarily will and what is involuntary such as character, the unconscious and the physical limitations of life itself. In this regard, human freedom involves an assent to that which is beyond and prior to freedom.

Ricoeur's first volume of collected essays appeared in 1955 under the title of *History and Truth*. Many of the pieces had already appeared in *Esprit*, a journal dedicated to Christian socialist and pacifist ideas. In various capacities, he would be associated with this journal for the most part of his professional career. The central issue in *History and Truth* concerns the antinomy that Ricoeur sees between history and truth but it ends with a tacit critique of Sartre's negative existentialism. During the same year Ricoeur would make the first of many trips to lecture in the United States. At the invitation of Quakers first met at Chambon-sur-Lignon, he visited Haverford College in Pennsylvania. This was followed by a trip to China on behalf of the French Ministry of Education.

In 1956, Ricoeur was called away from provincial life and invited to take up a position in Paris at the Sorbonne. Moving to a suburb in the south of the city, he established his family in a residential community founded by Mounier in 1939.

This was an intense period for many reasons. Ricoeur, an opponent of communism, found the intellectual and cultural life of Paris dominated by a doctrinaire – Stalinist – form of communism. It was hardly difficult to be labeled a fascist for the slightest opposition to the political spirit of the day. "What is more," Ricoeur reports, "not having been initiated into Parisian life, not being an alumnus of the Rue d'Ulm, ... I felt like a foreign body ... working mostly for myself, although I did have the impression of enjoying a fair hearing from the students" (CC 28).

A second installment of the *Philosophy of the Will* appeared in 1960 under the title *Finitude and Guilt*. It included two parts: *Fallible Man* and *The Symbolism of Evil*. Both works moved, in turn, further away from a singular phenomenological analysis. *Fallible Man* is Ricoeur's most concentrated effort toward a philosophical anthropology. It explains the human propensity toward evil – without humans actually being evil – by way of an ontology of disproportion. *The Symbolism of Evil* marks Ricoeur's hermeneutical turn. It attempts to study evil not by direct intuition or by use of deductive reasoning but by an interpretation of the experience of evil as it is objectively expressed in symbols and myths.

War interrupted Ricoeur's life again when he spoke out with many others to oppose France's military intervention in Algeria in the early 1960s. On one occasion he was temporarily detained and put under house arrest for several weeks. For the duration of the conflict the Ricoeur family lived cautiously for fear of retaliation by an ultraright secret group, the same group that would later attempt to assassinate General De Gaulle.

During this same period intellectual and popular interest in Husserl and Martin Heidegger (1889-1976) began to wane. The ideas of Sigmund Freud (1856-1939) and Ferdinand de Saussure (1857-1913) came into prominence along with the rising notoriety of structuralist arguments. This ushered in a new chorus line of popular intellectuals that would dominate the cultural limelight for the next twenty years. These included Claude Lévi-Strauss (b. 1908) (anthropology), Jacques Lacan (1901-1981) (psychoanalysis), Roland Barthes (1915-1980) (literary criticism) and Louis Althusser (1918-1990) (Marxism). Instead of embracing such a trend Ricoeur would continue to pursue his own unique form of analysis by deepening the productive relationship between phenomenology and hermeneutics. *Freud and Philosophy: An*

8

Essay in Interpretation was published in 1965. The work received a hostile reaction from Jacques Lacan and his followers. It was also during this period that Ricoeur would purposely confront structuralism in general and find himself ostracized from the popular intellectual currents of the day in a rather brusque and unjust manner.[5] In one notable instance Michel Foucault (1926-1984) refused to socially converse with Ricoeur.[6]

Not all of Ricoeur's engagements with famous intellectuals of the day were as dramatic. Even though their positions remained fundamentally opposed to one another, fruitful dialogues took place between Ricoeur and Claude Lévi-Strauss, and the specialist in semiotics, A. Julien Greimas (1917-1992) (CC 78-80). In 1969, Ricoeur published his second volume of collected essays entitled *The Conflict of Interpretations: Essays in Hermeneutics*. The various essays chart much of his thinking that guided him toward his "hermeneutic turn" and led to the publication of *Freud and Philosophy*.

In a more practical field of engagement Ricoeur had openly voiced his complaints on several occasions concerning the inefficiency and inappropriate conditions that prevailed in the French university system. He left the Sorbonne in the late sixties to participate in an experimental environment at the University of Paris at Nanterre. Unfortunately, even here, there was no escape from the turmoil and anxiety caused by the violent student demonstrations that swept the country in 1968. One year after the unrest ended Ricoeur was elected Dean of the Faculty of Letters. A short while later provocative maoists, communists and students of other political stripes confronted the police and turned the campus into a veritable battlefield. Ricoeur resigned his position the next year and requested a leave from his teaching post. This marked the beginning of a self-imposed exile from the French intellectual milieu for almost fifteen years.[7]

Following his resignation Ricoeur embraced a rigorous international teaching schedule with part of the year being spent at the University of Chicago in the United States and the other part at the Catholic University of Louvain in Belgium. As his connections to the French intellectual scene became more distant Ricoeur lectured internationally, especially in America. He also began to receive a number of honorary degrees from institutions world-wide. Many of his articles began to appear in English and most were published outside France.

In the early 1970s, Ricoeur combined his interests in symbolic language, interpretation and the creativity of language by concentrating on the problem of metaphor. *The Rule of Metaphor: Multi-Disciplinary*

Studies of the Creation of Meaning in Language appeared in 1975. In this work Ricoeur asserts that metaphors are more than just tropes of language and he details their power to redescribe the world. The use of metaphor suspends the first-order reference of ordinary language and opens the way for a second-order reference in which the world is manifested – no longer as an ensemble of objects to be manipulated but as an horizon of our own life and projects. The upshot of the work defends language as being more than a closed system of immanent relations and reveals that poetic language indeed has a referent. The work also revealed Ricoeur's great familiarity with American analytic and Anglo-Saxon philosophy and gained him great respect in the English-speaking world. In France the book received generally poor reviews. Its topic was out of vogue with the post-structuralist popularity of Foucault and it was critical of France's newest popular philosopher, Jacques Derrida (b. 1930). In the final chapter of the book Ricoeur argues against Derrida's insistence that some metaphors, like heliotrophic ones, have a predominant value in philosophical discourse.

After returning to the University of Paris in 1973, Ricoeur retained his international responsibilities at the Divinity School of the University of Chicago where he succeeded the famous Protestant theologian Paul Tillich (1886-1965). In Paris, Ricoeur assumed the directorship of the Center for Phenomenological and Hermeneutical Studies. He officially retired from the University of Paris in 1980 while continuing to teach in Chicago until 1991.

It was not until the publication of his multi-volume work, *Time and Narrative* (1983-5) that Ricoeur once again struck a chord with the French intellectual milieu. The central thesis of this work is that the time expressed in narrative is neither an objective, homogeneous cosmological time nor is it a subjectively lived psychological time; rather, it is a third – humanized – type of time. "Time becomes human time to the extent that it is organized after the manner of a narrative; narrative, in turn, is meaningful to the extent that it portrays the features of temporal experience" (TN1 3). A key theme to arise at the end of this analysis concerns "narrative identity." Our identities - both individually and communally – can only be grasped by interpreting the narratives of our existence that structures our temporal being.

In 1986, many of his lectures and articles first published outside France were released under the title *From Texts to Action: Essays in Hermeneutics II*. These essays trace out how Ricoeur extends the notion of textuality to all objectifications of life. Each of our lives becomes, so to speak, a quasi-text such that, like a text, our life embodies a meaning that can be made explicit through interpretation. Only in this way do we come to a more full understanding of what it means to be an acting human being.

In the same year Ricoeur delivered the famous Gifford Lectures in Edinburgh, Scotland. The outcome of this honor was the publication in 1990 of *Oneself as Another*. This text is an ambitious attempt to present a "hermeneutics of the self" with three latter chapters comprising what Ricoeur calls his "little ethics." The text follows a dense analytic-reflective structure on the question of action as it is given to description, narration and prescription. The whole hermeneutic is governed by the question who: who speaks? who acts? who tells a story? and who is the subject of moral imputation?

Ricoeur wrote an "Intellectual Autobiography" (PR) that appeared in 1995. In it he describes in detail the themes, influences and chronology of his philosophical journey. Published at the same time was a set of essays under one title *The Just*. The central theme is the judiciary. In its preoccupation with rights and laws the judiciary is a midway point between politics and moral philosophy. The judiciary is seen as an interpretative space where conflicts become enframed textually in the form of trials and hearings and thereby provide a model of how violence can be supplanted by rational arguments and their interpretation.[8]

One of Ricoeur's professional objectives has been to elaborate a methodological hermeneutics that can contribute to a multidisciplinary dialogue with the human sciences. While numerous articles from his large bibliography attest to this objective, two full-length works appeared in 1998. They are co-authored by Ricoeur with experts in their respective fields of biblical exegesis and neuroscience.[9]

In 2000, Ricoeur published *La Mémoire, l'histoire, l'oubli*.[10] The work attempts to fill a conceptual gap left in the wake of *Time and Narrative* and *Oneself as Another*. In these latter texts temporal experience and the role of narrative are discussed in the absence of both memory and forgetting. Ricoeur emphasizes the importance of "a just political memory." Such a memory must seek a balance between an "official" collective memory that is often ideologically motivated and the testimony of the witnesses – even when the last one has disappeared. Ricoeur is worried about official history and its penchant for "too much memory here, and too much forgetting there." Justice to the past and justice for the future can only be maintained by a critical relationship between a fidelity to memory and the truth of history.

Perspectives

In a recent presentation Ricoeur called to mind two formulae that summarize his attempt to understand how language and its large units of discourse (texts) mediate between lived experience and philosophical reflection.[11] The first, "symbol gives rise to thought," mentioned above, concludes his philosophy of will in the early 1960s. The second, "to explain more is to understand better," initiates a theme that transverses his works up until the present. To further these introductory remarks this latter formula will be elaborated with reference to philosophical anthropology.

Ricoeur has characterized his philosophy as a "philosophical anthropology." This project should not be confused with classical anthropology and its concern with *man*. Ricoeur is impassioned with revealing the limits of *capable man* (*homo capax*) (OA 181; PR 545; TJ 24).[12] By this he means an on-going attempt to uncover the human capacity to act and to assume responsibility for those actions. In a late work Ricoeur suggests that there are three ways of speaking about action. It can be described, which is the task of the human sciences and Anglo-American theories of action. Action can also be recounted or narrated. Lastly, it can be imputed with value and judged as good or bad. For didactic purposes Ricoeur summarized this "polysemy of action" under the triadic designation of description, narration, and prescription (OA 20, 152). The designation clearly describes the web of relations that must be determined to understand how we come to view practical actions as potentially ethical ones or, more succinctly, how we move from talking about human action in the practical field to speaking as moral agents in the ethical field.

Central to this triad is the fact that description, narration and prescription are three modes of language to speak about human action. Ricoeur's philosophical anthropology lies at the intersection of the problem of language and the problem of action. To describe this *mélange* of problems Ricoeur will sometimes employ the phrase, "poetics of action." The term "poetics," borrowed from Aristotle, generally denotes for Ricoeur the creative act of configuration that is in fact a creative reconstruction of experience in a literary mode. The creative aspect of compositions of all sorts is driven by the interplay of imagination and language. Thanks to our creative capacity to plot, to re-create and to metaphorically re-state experience, "we are prepared to look at human beings in a new way" (RI 84).

What changes for us in this interplay of the productive imagination and language – under the auspices of metaphor – is our way of dwelling in the world. Each configuration offers a new way of orienting ourselves in how we understand the world. In this sense, texts of many kinds are heuristic; that is, they have the capacity to open and unfold new dimensions of reality by means of inviting us, the reader, to suspend belief in an earlier description (FT 175). Owing to this interplay of imagination and language to create and re-create we discover reality itself in the process of being created. We begin to see reality in terms of potentialities and not in terms of actualities (RI 456-462). In light of Ricoeur's overall anthropology, action and language come together in this "poetic" dimension as a disclosure of possibility (RI 490).

The arguments that brought Ricoeur to such a position are of important note. In the 1970s, he published a series of studies (collected in FT) arguing that human action could be understood much in the same way as we understand texts. The argument was built around a dispute in the history of hermeneutics between "explanation" and "understanding." One camp argued that by ignoring the reader and author and focusing on the immanent system and patterns in the text alone that a text could be *explained* in a detached and objective manner, much like any other object studied in the natural sciences. The other camp insisted that the human sciences were quite distinct from natural science. They argued for the immediate *understanding* of texts by intuitively recapturing the original intention of the author. Ricoeur shortened the distance between these two camps by proposing a dialectic between explanation and understanding. He showed how "'explanation' (*Erklären*) requires 'understanding' (*Verstehen*) and brings forth in a new way the inner dialectic that constitutes 'interpretation' as a whole" (FT 163). This mediation of explanation and understanding in the process of text interpretation becomes the central hermeneutical problem for Ricoeur.

Key to this dialectic is the reader. Understanding a text is not complete until *a reader understands* the kinds of things the text is about, that is, until a reader appropriates "the depth semantics of the text and makes it his or her 'own'" (FT 167). Where explaining brings out the structure, that is, the internal static relations of the text, interpretation follows the path of thought opened up by the text (FT 18). Interpretation invites the reader "to place oneself en route toward the *orient* of the text" in order to understand better (FT 122). A text opens an ensemble of references; it opens a world freed from the limits of ostensive references. To understand a text is to light up our own situation – to understand oneself better – by entering a world freed from the particularity of what we think the world to be. Ricoeur's attempt to understand human existence converges with his hermeneutical method in the notion of appropriation.

> By 'appropriation,' I understand this: that the interpretation of a text culminates in the self-interpretation of a subject who thenceforth understands himself better, understands himself differently, or simply begins to understand himself. ... In short, in hermeneutical reflection – or in reflective hermeneutics – the constitution of the *self* is contemporaneous with the constitution of *meaning* (FT 118-9).

Ricoeur is keen to emphasize that understanding through appropriation is mediated by the explanatory procedures that preceded it and accompany it. It has nothing to do with some state of feeling or an emotional identification with the mental intention of the author. It has everything to do with the dynamic meaning released by the explanation insofar as a text has the power to disclose a world. This constant back and forth movement between an analytical-style explanation and an understanding open to interpretation is what Ricoeur identifies as the hermeneutical circle (FT 167). This circle is the insuperable structure of knowledge when it is applied to human things. The very fact that it involves a personal commitment, that is, appropriation on part of the reader, keeps the circle from being a vicious one. What must be kept in mind is that the act of reading is the crucial moment of the entire analysis. On this act rests the ability of the narratives, and poetic language in general, to transfigure the experience of the reader. Every text that we have read, understood and loved invites us to act and behave differently. Explanation and understanding are therefore two complementary parts in a single interpretative process. Ricoeur encapsulates the search for meaning and this interpretative process by the formula "to explain more is to understand better" (TN1 x).

Influences

It is very difficult to summarize the various influences that brought Ricoeur to pursue such deep and rich sets of analyses. In almost any one of his major works one will find intricate dialogues with a staggering number of thinkers from every tradition in Western philosophy. While both Aristotle and Emmanuel Kant figure prominently in these dialogues there are more immediate influences that can be sketched in to show the early informative environment that spawned Ricoeur's philosophical perspectives.

Ricoeur began his philosophical training in the 1930s at a time when the study of Hegel, Husserl and Heidegger were becoming central to an academic education. It signaled a shift away from the Cartesian/Kantian orthodoxy of the day and its concern with the identity of the rational and sensible subject. But Ricoeur will never entirely absolve himself of the *reflexive* paradigm that informs much of French philosophy since Descartes. By reflexive philosophy Ricoeur means a way of thinking that can be traced from Descartes' meditations on the *cogito* through to the rise of French neo-Kantian philosophy. It is a philosophy whose central concern is the possibility of self-understanding achieved by first understanding a subject's ability to know, to will, to evaluate and so forth.

> Reflexion is that act of turning back upon itself by which a subject grasps, in a moment of intellectual clarity and moral responsibility, the unifying principle of the operations among which it is dispersed and forgets itself as subject. 'The "I think,"' says Kant, 'must be able to accompany all my representations' (FT 12).

The weakness of reflexive philosophy is its inability to show exactly how the "I think," or the subject as a thinking subject, recognizes the self. From his earliest studies Ricoeur was made suspicious of explanations that argued for absolute transparency between the subject and its cognitive abilities or for any other such coincidence of the self with itself (PR 4). The danger of such transparency is that it makes consciousness of self an absolute and indubitable knowledge and eventually becomes the fundamental form of any positive knowledge. Consequently, from the outset, Ricoeur is "opposed to any philosophy of the Cartesian type based on the transparency of the ego to itself, and to all philosophy ... based on the self-positing of that ego."[13] Instead he pursues a *reflective* process that leads back indirectly to the self through an analysis of how the self manifests or objectifies itself in language, action and narrative. Ricoeur's future hermeneutical project therefore is a radical transformation of reflexive philosophy in that any knowledge of the self is never immediate – it must be both discovered and recovered.

At the Sorbonne Ricoeur found a more contemporary version of reflexive philosophy in the guise of Husserl's phenomenology. Despite the notoriety for his translation of Husserl's *Ideas I*, Ricoeur was never an uncritical disciple of the German thinker. Husserl believed that he could remove consciousness from the contingency of the natural world by mapping out a transcendental subjectivity separate from empirical consciousness and, in doing so, sought to achieve a transcendental knowledge that would be self-grounding and certain of itself. The result is the transcendental constitution of the subject that posits an immediate and intuitive consciousness of the self. The resulting ego is a foundational ego with its own self-immanence becoming the only indubitable point of reference. It becomes "an egology without ontology" (HA 194) with the constituent activity of consciousness being made absolute. In other words it becomes a form of subjective idealism – the very thing Ricoeur wished to avoid (HS 101ff).

Ricoeur recognized very quickly that Husserl's analysis brought about an irrevocable oblivion of the subject's rootedness in the world. Under the constraints of Husserl's egology all otherness is reduced to the monadic life of the ego. "The 'vanity' of the ego is stretched like a veil over the very being of its existence" (HA 232). In the end, the real existence of others, things and history are brought into doubt. The monadic ego cannot constitute "the Other" and cross the threshold to intersubjectivity (HA 195).

While Ricoeur will apply a version of the phenomenological analysis in his early study of the will, any remnant of such an analysis becomes less evident over the course of his future works. Instead, Ricoeur will critically endorse the initiatives of Martin Heidegger, Maurice Merleau-Ponty (1908-1961) and even the later Husserl in seeing that consciousness, bounded temporally, finds itself always already included in an intersubjective world whose significations encompass it and yet elude it at the same time. Meaning as such is no longer something that appears to my consciousness first and foremost, rather, it is something that must be wrestled from the world around me. Following the lead of Hans-Georg Gadamer (b. 1900), this meant taking phenomenology beyond pure reflection toward a phenomenological hermeneutics of interpretation. Ricoeur justified this graft of hermeneutics onto phenomenology by arguing that both fields in fact belong together – *"phenomenology remains the unsurpassable presupposition of hermeneutics ...* [and] *... phenomenology cannot constitute itself without a hermeneutical presuppositon"* (FT 26).

Ricoeur found the necessary support for his dramatic shift toward hermeneutics in the works of another reflexive philosophy, that of Jean

Nabert (1881-1960). For Nabert, existence and being are tied up in the act of becoming. This effort to exist and to be finds its source in an originating act the meaning of which human beings attempt to recuperate. This meaning cannot be grasped immediately in an act of intellectual intuition but discloses itself in signs, objects and acts that demand both analysis and interpretation. Further, Nabert showed how the figure of evil rends being so intensely that a subject can no longer retake possession of itself. Evil is confronted in acknowledging the anterior nature of this originating affirmation that characterizes existence.

At the same time Ricoeur was introduced to Husserl's ideas he came into contact with Gabriel Marcel (1889-1973). Ricoeur participated in Marcel's weekly "Friday" seminars that encouraged "secondary reflection" – a method that takes experience seriously before theory and the appeal to authority rob them of their original, affirmative power. It was Marcel who argued that the real task of philosophy was to deal with certain intractable "mysteries" about existence that could not be reduced to problems and easily dismissed by logical analysis. Marcel is famous for the distinction he drew between the lived body and the body-object, that is, my body as my own, as the living center of my experience, and that same body being regarded as a neutral object open for objective analysis. The relationship between these two notions cannot be reduced into an ideal object and understood rationally without destroying the fundamental experience of our incarnate experience. Marcel argued that there exists an underlying unity to such subject-object relationships that is the very source of the philosophical endeavor itself. Another Marcellian theme is that the other is already present in the first surging forth of existence. In any affirmation of my own existence, the existence of the other is co-affirmed. Like the body, this *coesse* of the other with myself is non-problematizable. It is mystery. All of these themes – problem-mystery distinction, the positing of an underlying unity to subject-object relations, and co-existence – will indelibly mark much of Ricoeur's thought.

Another influence of note in Ricoeur's early formation is the philosophy of *existenz* of Karl Jaspers (1883-1969). *Existenz* is the term that Jaspers uses to define the mode of authentic existence for the individual when one moves beyond a rational or scientific objectification of the self and existence. This authentic existence is characterized by freedom, infinite possibilities, loneliness and responsibilities. Such freedom is not unlimited. It is contoured by "boundary situations" such as death, suffering, guilt, chance and conflict. Given his great emphasis on freedom and responsibility, Jaspers sees human finitude burdened by the constant threat of failure and the incipient weight of guilt. The whole pallor of existence is therefore one of tragedy. What will attract Ricoeur's attention is Jaspers' attempt to give life some sense of certitude and order beyond the tragic dimension of our finitude. For Jaspers, just because beings may stumble under the weight of their failures it does not mean that ciphers of hope cannot be detected. Existence itself must be deciphered to find the courage to live with the inevitable failure of our projects and plans. Such a decipherment however is always indirect and enigmatic. The need to look at external ciphers of existence in order to find some revelation of transcendence will figure heavily in Ricoeur's later work on symbols and texts.

There is one last influence important to mention. Throughout the course of his professional career Ricoeur has never hidden his biblical faith (HT 5). On the other hand, he has consistently attempted to pursue a path that brackets his religious convictions in order to protect the autonomy of his philosophical discourse. While admitting "that at the deep level of motivations" such convictions might have some effect on the interest he takes in a problem, Ricoeur believes his arguments "do not assume any commitment from the reader to reject, accept, or suspend anything with regard to biblical faith" (OA 24). In the meantime Ricoeur has made a substantial contribution to contemporary theology. Many terms peculiar to his thought such as "hermeneutics of suspicion," "second naïveté" and "conflict of interpretation" have become commonplace in present theological discourse.[14]

Endnotes

1. Frans D. Vansina, ed., *Paul Ricoeur, Primary and Secondary Bibliography* (Leuven, Belgium: Leuven University Press and Peeters, 2000).
2. Ricoeur nuances this philosophic hope as a form of "post-Hegelian Kantianism;" see CI 412; TN3 215, 226, 323, 329; FT 197-202, CC 83. For a discussion of what such a designation implies see Pamela Sue Anderson, *Ricoeur and Kant: Philosophy of the Will* (Atlanta, Georgia: Scholars Press, 1993) and John W. Van Den Hengel, *The Home of Meaning: The Hermeneutics of the Subject of Paul Ricoeur* (Washington, D.C.: University Press of America, 1982), 214ff.

3. Charles E. Reagan, *Paul Ricoeur: His Life and His Works* (Chicago: The University of Chicago Press, 1996) 133.

4. See Charles E. Reagan, *Paul Ricoeur: His Life and His Works.* François Dosse's more comprehensive *Paul Ricoeur: Les sens d'une vie* (Paris: Éditions La Découverte, 1997) has yet to be translated into English.

5. François Ewald, "Paul Ricoeur: un parcours philosophique," *Magazine Littéraire* Nr. 390, September 2000, 20-26.

6. As described in Didier Eribon, *Michel Foucault*, trans. Betsy Wing (Cambridge, Massachusetts: 1991) 189-190.

7. Charles Reagan, *Paul Ricoeur*, 41.

8. A second volume, *Le Juste II*, will be published in 2001; another work, *On Authority*, is forthcoming from Routledge.

9. André Lacocque and Paul Ricoeur, *Thinking Biblically: Exegetical and Hermeneutical Studies*, trans. David Pellauer (Chicago: University of Chicago Press, 1998) and Jean-Pierre Changeux and Paul Ricoeur, *What Makes Us Think?* trans. M. B. DeBevoise (Princeton, N.J.: Princeton University Press, 2000).

10. Paul Ricoeur, *La Mémoire, l'histoire,l'oubli* (Paris: Seuil, 2000).

11. Paul Ricoeur, "Synthèse Panoramique." Presentation made on receiving the 1999 Balzan Prize for Philosophy in Berne, Switzerland.

12. Paul Ricoeur in "A Response by Paul Ricoeur," in *Paul Ricoeur and Narrative: Context and Contestation*, ed. Morny Joy (Calgary: University of Alberta Press, 1997), xxxix.

13. Paul Ricoeur, in the "Forword" to Don Ihde, *Hermeneutic Phenomenology: The Philosophy of Paul Ricoeur* (Evanston: Northwestern University Press, 1971), xv.

14. Ricoeur's central theological contributions can be followed by consulting the theological text cited in note 9 and Paul Ricoeur, *Essays in Biblical Interpretation,* ed. Lewis S. Mudge (Philadelphia: Fortress Press, 1980). See also Paul Ricoeur, *Figuring the Sacred: Religion, Narrative and Imagination*, ed. Mark I. Wallace, trans. David Pellauer (Minneapolis: Fortress Press, 1995); Paul Ricoeur, *L'herméneutique biblique*, ed. and trans. by François-Xavier Amherdt (Paris: Les Éditions du Cerf, 2001). For a summary of Ricoeur's theological contributions see Kevin J. Vanhoozer, *Biblical Narrative in the Philosophy of Paul Ricoeur: A Study in Hermeneutics and Theology* (Cambridge: Cambridge University Press, 1990).

2
The Early Works:
The Will, Fallibility
and Evil

Freedom and Nature

Ricoeur's first original philosophical work, *Philosophy of the Will*
(1950) was a projected three-volume study loosely modeled on Jaspers'
three-volume *Philosophy* (1932). Each volume proposed to study the
act of willing in light of a particular descriptive mode. These were to
include an eidetic, an empiric and a poetic description. Published ten
years apart only the first two volumes have ever appeared. Ricoeur
suggests that the third installment, the promised "poetics of the will,"
has been fulfilled in part by the combination of works that have
appeared since the 1960s (PR 14).

The first volume, *Freedom and Nature: The Voluntary and the
Involuntary* attempts to apply Husserl's method of phenomenological
(eidetic) reduction to the theme of incarnate existence first described by
Marcel. Ricoeur's choice of the will as the theme of his first
philosophical project is a critique of the implicit belief that we can
assimilate such human functions as feeling and willing into our
objective knowledge of reality (FN 16). For Ricoeur incarnate
existence "overflows the objectivity" which the intellect can apply to it.
Expressions of the will are "a living experience in which we are

submerged more than signs of mastery which our intelligence exercises over our human condition" (FN 17).

In studying the will as a wellspring of motives both known and unknown Ricoeur hopes to show indirectly the impotence of the *cogito* to posit its own foundation and to be self-contained. This impotence is never more visible than when the *cogito* collides with what Ricoeur will call the involuntary aspects of human existence. What becomes immediately apparent is that the source of human freedom is not found in the *cogito*. Freedom can only be understood by what constraints it and these constraints lie outside the power of the *cogito* to constitute them. The root of the problem is that consciousness can never capture the living unity of existence. The appearance of "consciousness is always ... the disruption of an intimate harmony" that "recoils from the reality of ... body and of objects." It replaces the spontaneity of existence with its own delusions of being "ideally complete, transparent, and capable of positing itself absolutely" (FN 17-18).

A study of the will, therefore, is a "limited contribution" to understand the mystery of reconciliation or restoration "of the original concord of vague consciousness with its body and its world" (FN 18). This original concord is never re-achieved. Consciousness is discovered to be both disruption and bond. The structures of willing themselves will be seen to be ones of rupture as well as of union.

The will in this sense is a mediation between what it actively wills and what restricts such willing. It is this mediation of the active will and its restrictions that moves the question of free will beyond the classical dualism of free-will and determinism to situate it in a being who is in conflict with itself.

By interpreting freedom with respect to what is involuntary and voluntary in the will, freedom becomes a limit concept, that is, something that cannot be known in itself. It will act as a background or horizon of unity that brings this rupture or dualism of existence into focus (FN 484; PA 19). As a limit concept it will restrict our claims to knowledge of a purely free will.

The first task necessary to grasp the reciprocal relationship between the voluntary and involuntary is to distinguish such a relationship from the natural articulations of willing (FN 6). This is achieved by describing the will in a phenomenological manner. Such a description entails submitting the will to an *eidetic* reduction where the common, everyday understanding of the will is bracketed out. The hope is to leave out the concrete life of the will in order to expose in an ideal way the pure functions of the will that include choice, action and consent.

What Ricoeur wants to reach is the neutral realm of pure possibilities of the will. In a later work Ricoeur remarked that he wanted to sketch in "the neutral sphere of man's most fundamental possibilities, or as it were, the undifferentiated keyboard upon which guilty as well as the innocent man might play" (FM xvi).

As such, this will not be a psychological study. An eidetic reduction brackets or holds in suspension all ontological assumptions and empirical meanings normally applied to the will. It also excludes from specific consideration two important aspects of human existence – the fault and Transcendence. The fault is an idiosyncratic term used by Ricoeur to denote the basic intuition that a basic disruption – a break, tear or rift – marks all of human existence. It is the awareness that our existence is somehow innately flawed. This is the awareness depicted by so many symbols of evil, fall and inescapable labyrinths of passions in bondage. It is "the presence of an absolute irrational in the heart of man" that is opaque to intelligibility (FN 24-25). Ricoeur believes that the fault has to be abstracted in order to uncover the primordial possibilities of the will. For the very same reason the eidetic reduction also abstracts or brackets Transcendence, the answer to the fault.

> In suspending the fault and Transcendence, that is, bondage and inspiration, I can give full due to the experience of responsibility. ... This pure experience already represents a break in the circle which I form with my self; freedom transcends itself already in the body. Thanks to the abstraction ... it is possible to restore the meaning of freedom understood as a dialogue with nature. Such abstraction is necessary in order to understand ... the paradox and the mystery of incarnate freedom (FN 33).

The end of the such intense bracketing reveals three fundamental functions of the will: "I decide" (choice), "I move my body" (motion or action) and "I consent" (consent). In each case voluntary and involuntary elements coexist.

Willing is stretched out towards the future by its projects. In the first modality of willing, *choice,* I am turned toward a "something to be done" that is categorically different from that of wish or desire. "I determine *myself* to the extent that I determine myself *to* ..." (PA 5). A choice or decision specifies in outline a future action as my own action, as an action lying in my power. But a project unifies my existence in a given moment only because it takes root in what is involuntary in my life. There are no decisions apart from motivations. The irruption of choice is a discontinuity in the web of possible motivations (FN 180). If a motivation is based on values that are not invented but encountered, then the irruption of choice is the voluntary aspect of the will that transcends the involuntary "*affective indistinctness of motives*" (FN 129). In the moment of choice and decision "motivation expresses very clearly ... one of the hinges of the voluntary and involuntary" (PA 6). Another hinge is "the corporeal involuntary." My decision to walk across the Gobi Desert or swim the English Channel must be seen with regard to the limits of my body. Such feats are never entered upon without considering the restrictions imposed by the very condition of our existence, like the body. Such involuntary conditions frame our possible range of voluntary motivations (FN 93ff).

A similar condition exists with respect to *motion*, the second mode of willing. Every time I move my body and decide to move or act I meet certain resistances and must exert an effort to effect the decision. Ricoeur identifies three such involuntary resistances: performed skills (involuntary spontaneity of the body), emotion and habit (FN 231ff). In every instance the will either uses them or succumbs to them as a degradation of its own willing activity.

The third mode of willing, *consent,* is defined as an adaptation to necessity or to the absolute involuntary. These include character (understood as the stable and absolutely unchosen figure of the existing being), the unconscious (a zone forever inconvertible into actual consciousness) and life (the fact that birth is an unpremeditated gift and death an unavoidable reality). Character, the unconscious and life inextricably bind each of us to the finite and to the contingent. Consequently, the demeanor of consent is one of sorrow and anxiety over unchangeable necessities that we cannot master. But consent does no more than identify the necessities which structure willing. It does not coalesce with necessity.

> Consent to necessity is never achieved. Who can accept himself without qualification, concretely, daily? It is here that suffering acquires its philosophical significance, as the impossibility of coincidence with oneself; it introduces into the self a specific negativity, in the sense that necessity is now lived not as affecting, but as wounding: I am not at home in my own nature (PA 17).

In the very least then there is no unity or synthesis of the voluntary and involuntary. The paradoxical relationship of freedom and necessity remains a scandal to the intellect. Reflection cannot repair the rift. It cannot be repaired, Ricoeur reminds us, because there is "a secret wound" inscribed in the human act of existing. There is a rent or "a lesion in being itself" that makes life as much willed as it is endured (FN 444). At most there are only "ways of consent" (stoic, orphic, hope) that accommodate the will to its situation. Consent is the human but disquiet link between freedom and nature. "It represents converting, within myself, the hostility of nature into the freedom of necessity. Consent is the asymptotic progress of freedom towards nature" (FN 346).

Ricoeur concludes that "freedom is not a pure act, it is, in each of its moments, activity and receptivity. It constitutes itself in receiving what it does not produce: values, capacities, and sheer nature" (FN 484). The nuance should not be lost here. The involuntary aspects of human willing have no meaning of their own (FN 5). Their intelligibility is a function of the fact that human beings exert the will in deciding, acting and consenting. What we understand to be our freedom of the will can only be defined in contrast to what limits it. It is such involuntary constraints that incarnate human freedom. As such, our freedom issues from our act of willing. Since our willing takes place in time and space based on our own biological limitations we should never expect it to meet the ideal of an omniscient rational or creative freedom. Any conceived synthesis of the voluntary and the involuntary acts as no more than a limit idea. It is in this sense that Ricoeur concludes that we live by "a freedom which is human and *not* divine, of a freedom which does not posit itself absolutely because it is *not* Transcendence. To will is not to create" (FN 486).

Fallibility

The second volume of *Philosophy of the Will* is entitled *Finitude and Guilt* and consists of two parts, *Fallible Man* and *The Symbolism of Evil*. Both works address the same question: if our freedom is a merely human freedom, and there is nothing in the fundamental structures of such freedom that determines its misuse, then why do humans misuse their freedom? In different terms Ricoeur wants to elaborate what structures of human being would account "for the weakness of a being exposed to evil and capable of doing wrong, but not of actually being evil" (PR 15).

Fallible Man is perhaps the most appreciated and most studied of

Ricoeur's early philosophy of the will.[1] It is also his most sustained effort in detailing a philosophical anthropology. The work is intended to be an *empirics* of the will that would study aspects of willing and freedom bracketed out in the eidetic analyses of *Freedom and Nature*. While *Freedom and Nature* helped to identify the *essential* structures of our human being it did not provide a full understanding of human being. Even though this first analysis revealed human freedom as *essentially* incarnate by what we will, the study did not attempt to address our *actual* freedom as it is exposed to the disruptive conditions of existence. *Fallible Man* will specifically zero in on the problem of the fault that was excluded in the first study. He is not interested in uncovering "... the root origin of evil" but in giving a "description of the place where evil appears and from where it can be seen," namely, in human fallibility (FM xxiv).

While still a descriptive phenomenology, *Fallible Man* will be descriptive of existence as it is reflected through consciousness. Seen through consciousness the human capacity for evil will be rooted in the ambiguity of human existence. This ambiguity will be described in terms of an essential disproportion between finitude and the infinite at the heart of our being. It will shown how in every act of consciousness toward the object, the person and feeling we are caught in a dramatic mediation that attempts to construct a synthesis between what is finite in us and what is infinite.

Fallible Man begins with what Ricoeur calls the non-philosophical "precomprehension of 'misery.'" This is the theme of human division and brokeness that runs like a great thread through all the psalms, philosophies and literature that have catalogued it. Starting "from the Platonic myth representing the soul as a melange to the beautiful Pascalian rhetoric of two Infinities toward Kierkegaard's *Concept of Dread*" (FM 12) we come upon a pathos that marks our existence as essentially divided. The task is to bring this rhetoric or "*pathétique* of misery" to philosophic discourse, from *mythos* to *logos* (FM 26).

What the rhetoric of misery makes abundantly evident is that our humanity is marked by a fundamental disproportion – a certain non-coincidence – of self to self. This disproportion is the expression of our "unstable ontological constitution." It has nothing to do with being situated somewhere "between angel and animal" (FM 6). More to the point, human beings are a paradoxical mixture of the finite and the infinite. Finitude and infinitude are two modalites that belong to the totality of being human. Our very existence consists in mediating the disproportion between these two poles. Our unstable ontological constitution coexists with our ontological characteristic of "being-intermediate" (FM 6). To exist as human is to mediate. If the possibility of evil is to be understood at all, then it will be best observed in our nature as mediating beings. "Man's specific weakness and his essential fallibility are ultimately sought within this structure of mediation between the pole of his finitude and the pole of his infinitude" (FM xx).

Mediation is the attempt to hold the finite and infinite in a stable relationship by means of a synthesis. Such mediations can only be studied by breaking down the nebula of misery into distinct forms through pure reflection (FM 25). To achieve this Ricoeur will apply a *finite-[being-intermediary]-infinite* schema in order to expose the frailty of the syntheses we construct at all levels of existence. The three key syntheses – or zones of frailty – described in the course of *Fallible Man* are the transcendental synthesis (knowing), the practical synthesis (acting) and affectivity (feeling). Where the rhetoric of misery gives the pre-philosophical global view of our radical disproportion, each of the syntheses is a philosophical attempt to approximate this totality. But philosophical reflection cannot re-achieve this totality "because in man's precomprehension of himself there is a wealth of meaning which reflection is unable to equal" (FM 11). In order to address this residue of meaning Ricoeur will follow a much different approach in the second part, *The Symbolism of Evil*.

The Transcendental Synthesis

One would think that the first zone of frailty or synthesis of disproportion that Ricoeur would locate as part of a philosophical meditation on finitude would be in one's own body. It is in the body that finitude is so radically felt and acknowledged. Yet Ricoeur chooses to begin his transcendental reflection on what appears before us. Before I am directed toward my body I am directed toward the world, toward things and persons. He argues "it is 'upon' the *thing* that this reflection discerns the power of knowing, upon the thing that it discovers the specific disproportion of knowing, between receiving it and determining it. Upon the thing it apprehends the power of synthesis" (FM 28).

From the finite side, a human being always begins from his or her own perspective. Our perception is essentially finite. By the very limitations of our visual apparatus and other senses our field of vision never totally encompasses an object. While my body may open me to the world, perspective ultimately narrows this openness (FM 36). On the other hand, we have another relation to things. While we cannot perceive an object from every side and hence cannot see it in its totality, that same totality can still be signified. Signifying our relations to objects transcends the finitude of perception. "I say more than I see when I signify" (FM 44). The dialect of "perspective" and "name" is the very dialectic of finitude and infinitude. The infinite moment of naming and speaking is not in simple denomination but in the verb. Where the name transcends the seen, the verb transcends the name. The verb, in helping to hold together a sentence, bestows on human beings the power to deny or affirm something (FM 50). This correlation of affirmation and verb is a type of "supra-signification" because the verb implies two dimensions of truth: existential with reference to present time and relational with regard to the subject (FM 56).

At the level of knowing, therefore, a fundamental disproportion is uncovered "between the verb which gives expression to being and truth at the risk of falling into error, and, on the other hand, the passive look which is riveted to appearance and perspective" (FM 57). How do human beings effect mediation between these two poles? In reference to Kant, Ricoeur suggests that it is imagination that mediates speaking and looking or between meaning and appearance (FM 70). We are not conscious of this mediation at the level of transcendental synthesis. The consciousness referred to here takes place at a formal level – the Kantian "I think." It constitutes its own unity outside of itself on the object. It is consciousness in general, that is, the pure and simple project of the object – it is not yet the unity of the person in itself and for itself. It is not one person. "It is no one" (FM 70). Yet we cannot move from the *pathétique* of misery to a philosophic discourse without this step because the mediation between the infinite and the finite in things fundamentally expresses our mode of being-intermediary. The power of knowing is "man's most radical disproportion"(FM 10). It is radical because reflection does not start with myself but with the object before me and is mediated by something as unknowable in itself - the imagination (FM 64).

Practical Synthesis

Next, Ricoeur applies the *finite-[being-intermediary]-infinite* structure to the practical synthesis. He discloses a disproportion between character (finite pole) and our desire for totality (infinite pole) that finds its fragile mediation in respect toward the person.

The practical synthesis pertains to "the 'I will,' with its whole cycle of specific determinations: 'I desire,' 'I can,' etc." (FM 72). It is the will that involves the person in the totality of all that is. What narrows the will's involvement in totality is character. While our humanity opens us to all that is human – including its virtues and vices – our individual characters significantly narrows the realization of what is possible. Character for Ricoeur is "the radically non-chosen origin of all my choices" (FM 95). In character one finds desires, both limited and confused, that are beyond control but nonetheless are unique and singular to one person. Moreover, there are habits that contour action and responses thereby restricting "our field of availability" (FM 88). In short, the will, sifted through the grid of character with its desires and habits, limits the total field of possible human motivations and acts. As with perspective, character announces our finiteness and the unchosen conduit through which we exercise our freedom. On the other hand, to the degree that each of us is constrained by character we feel "destined to ... totality" (FM 7; 100). Ricoeur calls this infinite pole in the practical field happiness. As employed here happiness is not the sum of pleasures. It acts more like an end toward which our practical actions are only instrumental. Happiness is the horizon of fulfillment against which "the partial aims and disconnected desires of our life stand out" (FM 101).

What mediates this cleavage between the finitude of character and "the infinitude of happiness"(FM 103) is the person. This third term of the synthesis – the person – is primarily a project that I represent to myself. It is the ideal self. The term person stands for "the human quality of man" that makes a person a human person (FM 107). In this practical synthesis the person is not yet an experienced plenitude but an "'is to be'" (FM 110). In this sense the synthesis only comes to completion when respect draws out the person as an ethical object (FM 111). To the degree that no one character exceeds its bonds of finitude, respect has a feeling function, that of sympathy. To the degree that everyone's desire for fulfillment must be esteemed as my own, respect has a reasonable component. It is this combination of feeling and reason - always in conflict at the heart of our humanity - that make the practical synthesis a fragile one indeed.

Affective Fragility

The prior two analyses began with the object and the person. The last analysis in *Fallible Man* begins with feeling. This is the most lengthy and difficult analysis because philosophy cannot adequately objectify the disproportion buried *within* the heart of human beings. The *finite-[being-intermediary]-infinite* structure cannot be applied in the normal sense and expected to reach "the *life* of feeling" since

28

feeling is not something that appears before us (FM 138). "Feeling is the most intimate point of the person, the place where the disproportion is concentrated, the point of culmination or intensity in human fallibility" (PA 31). To pursue his analysis Ricoeur looks for a duality within the heart. He borrows the Platonic image of the heart, *Thumos*, as a zone of mediation between our basic desires (*epithumia*) (finite pole) and our spiritual desires (*Eros*) (infinite pole) that originate from the intellect and reason (FM 139). Where *epithumia* strives for pleasure *Eros* strives for happiness. Happiness here is not used formally as above. It is the happiness that issues from the core of our own being as real as we have desire for pleasure.

In a dense presentation Ricoeur describes how *Eros* borrows from *Thumos* and turns its thymic objects of desire and pleasures into symbols of desire. Like the ladder of love in Plato's *Symposium*, *Eros* (happiness) is able to hierarchize the various levels of pleasure in order to reveal itself as the greatest of pleasures (FM 150). "That is why I would readily speak of the schematization of happiness in the *élan* and in the objects of the ... [thumos]. One of those objects suddenly represents, in a kind of affective immediacy, the all of the desirable" (FM 198). Consequently, happiness becomes an object of desire (a feeling) in us, a desire that draws us beyond present pleasures toward a horizon of possibility. It is from this "affective figuration" of happiness in the *thumos* that human beings draw their "undefined restlessness" and spiritual desire (FM 199). Ricoeur will even speak of this feeling as having ontological dimensions becoming our "very openness to being" (FM 159).

To be sure, Ricoeur warns that the thymic objects borrowed to project happiness are symbolic. To take what we have and what temporal status and worth we might achieve as the "all" is to make them an idol. Such forgetting is "the source and occasion of every mistake and all illusion" (FM 199). The desire for happiness is the impassioned life built upon the pleasurable objects sought in our passional existence. The passional existence will find its fulfillment in the instantaneous satisfaction of pleasure whereas the impassioned life aspires to totality, to the perfection of happiness. This affective figuration toward happiness is a feeling that binds together what knowledge divides. Whereas the whole movement of rational knowledge tends to set the world against me, feeling seeks unity. It throws me out of myself toward the affection through which I feel myself existing.

29

Feeling alone, through its pole of infinitude, assures me that I can *'continue my existence in'* the openness of thinking and of acting; the originating affirmation is felt here as the Joy of 'existing in' the very thing which allows me to think and to act; then reason is no longer an other: I am it, you are it, because we are what it is (FM 209).

This last statement cannot be passed over quickly. In the practical synthesis above, the one where character and happiness were mediated through respect, happiness was defined abstractly and to some extent remained an "empty idea" (FM 140, 155). What this last synthesis reveals – at the level of feeling – is that *we are this desire* for happiness, unity and totality. Unlike the previous two mediations the affective synthesis interiorizes the duality that strikes at the heart of our humanity and dramatizes it as conflict. We are pierced by an "indefinite affective quest" marked by the sign of conflict. In short, "the self is conflict" (FM 201).

It should be evident that each mediation is characterized by tensions compounded by the demands of the opposing pole. There remains something incomplete in every attempt to mediate what we know, will and feel. What is incomplete however is fuelled by the fundamental disproportion, the "primordial conflict" that defines our human existence. It is this secret rift, this non-coincidence of self to self, that feeling reveals. Human beings remain torn (FM 216). But this is only the partial lesson to be taken from this form of analysis. As we learned from the analysis of the will any discourse on finitude can only be delineated by what limits it – in this case infinitude. In becoming aware of our finite points-of-view as finite points-of-view "a *movement* transgressing this finitude" is always already there (FM 39). As such, the infinite poles of the above syntheses are primary or originating (FM 208). In following the infinite pole of each synthesis (saying; the idea of happiness; the feeling of happiness) there is in an intensification of the realization that "Being is here affirmation, yes, joy. ... I am it and I participate in it" (FM 210). This means that the power of human being to know, to act and to feel reflects a deep longing for truth and happiness that cannot be totally negated by the various contingent experiences of our finite existence. Any reflection on these zones of frailty is "already combined with a procedure oriented toward the apprehension of the 'primary affirmation' by which I am constituted as a self over and above all my choices and individual acts" (FM xxvi). Human finitude, therefore, contains a seed, a deep "vehemence of the

Yes" that is not extinguished in the dark night of dread and anguish (FM 208).

This dialectic of originating affirmation and existential finitude is what make human beings fragile. "Man is the Joy of Yes in the sadness of the finite" (FM 215). Each synthesis, each task of mediation, only progressively manifested the fault or fundamental disproportion that defines human existence. Our inability to seize and censure this disproportion is not the call to failure or fate. It simply indicates the underlying condition of vulnerability and fallibility. There is nothing in the concept of fallibility that demands we act badly or misuse our freedom. That we do act badly is a fact but not one that can be predicted and deduced from what a rational reflection reveals about our human condition.

The Symbolism of Evil

The Symbolism of Evil is the last work published in Ricoeur's project *Philosophy of Will*. It moves away from charting what makes evil possible in human being to the reality of evil – "the whole riddle of the fault." Ricoeur has been careful not to confuse finitude with evil. Concerned with describing the essential structures of human being the most his philosophical reflection has achieved thus far are such concepts as finitude and fallibility, but not evil. Ricoeur is very aware right from the beginning that the problem of evil is an astonishing and scandalous phenomenon that confronts human consciousness. "Evil precedes my awareness [and] ... cannot be analyzed into individual faults" (CI 306). It is an involuntary conundrum at the very heart of the voluntary. Evil is an enigma that our conceptual systems cannot deduce, master or deny. It is the "reign of the already there" (CI 304).

The problem is further complicated by the fact that "there is no direct, nonsymbolic language of evil undergone, suffered, or committed" (CI 289). This turns into a "battle between thought and the symbolic." It becomes a question of how thought, once entering "into the *revealing* power of symbol," can develop along the line of rationality and rigor proper to philosophy. Owing to the enigma of evil Ricoeur foregoes the "backward flight" toward some ever-elusive "first truth" about evil. Instead he will note that historically evil is not completely ineffable. Both Hebraic and Hellenic literatures evince "the existential eruptions of this consciousness of fault" (SE 9). Ricoeur begins his meditation on symbols, therefore, from "the fullness of language and of meaning already there; it begins from within language which has already taken place and in which everything in a certain sense has already been said" (CI 287).

This starting point marks an important shift in Ricoeur's philosophical strategy where phenomenology is displaced by hermeneutics. In this early stage hermeneutics is simply a form of indirect thinking that no longer seeks evil in the fundamental structures of human being but in terms of existence, that is, as it expresses itself in language, especially the language of confession and myth.

Long before philosophy reflects rationally upon the mystery of evil generations of people have already confronted its reality in religious confession and in the symbolic language of myth. "Through confession the consciousness of fault is brought into the light of speech; through confession man remains speech, even in the experience of his own absurdity, suffering, and anguish" (SE 7). Instead of beginning with the familiar concept of original sin Ricoeur begins with the primitive language of avowal; "the confession of sins creates a language for itself by its very strangeness; the experience of being oneself but alienated from oneself gets transcribed immediately on the plane of language in the mode of interrogation" (SE 8).

In the symbolic language of confession three primary symbols of evil can be discovered: defilement, sin and guilt. Defilement, or stain, is the most objective of the three. It is the outward mark of evil from which one must be cleansed. Defilement is never identical with the physical stain. It is a quasi-material thing that resists reflection but nonetheless infects as a sort of filth and works upon our undividedly psychic and corporeal existence (SE 25). Sin, on the other hand, is the transgression of a rule or law that must be compensated for in some way. It is experienced in the feeling of fear and anguish owing to a loss of a bond (SE 71). Guilt or the guilty conscience is the more internal and subjective avowal of evil. It also brings us to a new level in the symbolism of evil since what is at stake is "the evil use of liberty, felt as an internal diminution of the value of the self"(SE 102).

Defilement, sin and guilt are not signs but symbols. A symbol is always opaque because its first primary or literal meaning points analogically toward a second one. This second meaning is latent, indirect and figurative but can only be apprehended through the first (CI 12). "The symbol is the movement of the primary meaning which makes us participate in the latent meaning and thus assimilates us to that which is symbolized without our being able to master the similitude intellectually" (SE 16). As such, symbols cannot be reduced to analogy or to any form of literalness. Their meaning is potentially "inexhaustible."

Taken together these primary symbols (defilement, sin, guilt) interpenetrate one another and orient themselves toward a particular horizon, namely, the concept of the servile will or perhaps better known as the bondage of the will (SE 151). Discussion of these symbols and concepts is only possible because of an abstraction that has uprooted them from the rich world of myths. To show the pervasiveness of these symbols and the concept of the servile will, Ricoeur proposes a type of exegesis on myths, "the medium for the living experience" of the fault (SE 161).

A myth is a symbolic narrative or symbol in the form of a story. Unlike previous periods, modern man that takes myth as myth because history and myth have become dissociated. We have come to live in historical time and no longer in mythical time. Ricoeur does not give a general theory of myth but limits himself to the investigation of myths of evil in Western culture. He identifies four basic types of myths (SE 175ff). First, there are the myths concerned with creation and the end of evil. A classical example would be the Sumero-Akkadian drama of creation called *Enuma elish*. In this type of myth evil is primordial with the very creation of the world. It is built into the story as is creation's salvation. "There is no history of salvation distinct from the drama of creation" (SE 191). Salvation can only be re-enacted in a ritual celebration in which people celebrate the overcoming of evil power and the birth of a new order and a new life. Next are the tragic myths of which the story of Prometheus is exemplary. In such myths evil is divided into an ambiguity between the wicked gods (Zeus' punishment) and a brash hero (Prometheus' theft of fire). Third, there are myths similar to the Orphic myth which recount the exile and the fall of a soul. They reveal the same pattern where the only way for the alienated soul to purify itself is by returning to its origins through some secret knowledge or *gnosis*. Lastly, there is the Adamic myth. Where the other myths are speculative and locate the origin of evil in a state or situation prior to human beings, the Adamic myth situates the origin of evil in the misuse of freedom by human beings. Therefore evil is historical, not primordial. This leads to the notion of an eschatological end of history.

Up to this point Ricoeur has been doing nothing more than excavating exegetically the wealth of symbolic meaning latent in the myths of evil. His real aim should we forget, is to glean whatever philosophical understanding is possible about human existence by following the indication of symbol. His next move is to go from a simple exegesis to a philosophy of myths. In other words, he wants to move *from symbol to thought* and in doing so he wishes to avoid falling back into a form of gnosticism or simply reducing myths to allegory (CI 299).

To achieve this Ricoeur pursues "a creative interpretation ... that would respect the original enigma of symbols, [and] let itself be taught by this enigma" (CI 300). This is done by putting all the classes of myth into a dynamic play against one dominant myth in order "to bring to light a circularity among the myths." While acknowledging a common thread that binds all the myths together so that one cannot be accepted and others rejected, pre-eminence is given to the Adamic myth (SE 309). This is done for several reasons but perhaps the most compelling is the presence of the symbol of the serpent. It stands for evil's other face and signifies that human beings do not begin evil. Evil is already there. "Beyond the projection of our own covetousness, the serpent stands for the tradition of an evil more ancient than man himself. The serpent is the *Other* of human evil" (CI 295; SE 313).

What this interpretative engagement with "the cycle of myths" reveals is an embattled world of symbols with no totality of comprehension under any one figure. In fact, this *Other* represented by the serpent exhausts our discursive powers to understand evil definitively. "No great philosophy of the *totality* is capable of giving an account ... of evil in a meaningful schema" (CI 311). On the other hand, the engagement was not without merit since it brought to the fore a "superabundance" or surplus of meaning. Since "the world of symbols is not tranquil" the hermeneutics of symbol provoked us to think more and permitted us to share in the battle where "the symbol's giving of meaning and the intelligent initiative of deciphering are bound together" (CI 298).

Ricoeur's wager is that "the symbol gives rise to thought" and in the to-and-fro of interpretation with the "the gift of meaning from symbol" the philosopher profits in understanding (SE 348). In the end even if the process of an interpretative hermeneutics is open ended and never exhausts the depth of meaning in the symbol we "shall have a better understanding of man and of the bond between the being of man and the being of all beings" (SE 355). As such, being "can still speak to me," not in the pre-critical form of immediate belief but as a second immediacy – a *second naïveté* – aimed at by hermeneutics (SE 352).

The Symbolism of Evil marks Ricoeur's hermeneutical turn in his thinking. The great lesson from this work was the recognition that our only access to the experience of evil is through symbolic expressions. Nothing is transparent about symbols. They are opaque and possess a double intentionality in which there is both a manifest and hidden meaning. Nonetheless symbols are interpreted through linguistic expressions and thereby are incorporated into "the fullness of language." It is to this "fullness of language" that Ricoeur will turn subsequently in hopes to better understand the human capacity for meaning and understanding. This will include not only the symbolic and mythic forms of language but the poetic and narrative as well.

While it might be argued that this methodological development terminates Ricoeur's interest in a philosophy of the will and phenomenology, it should be kept in mind that he will remain faithful to phenomenology's original inspiration that the intentional meaning of consciousness resides outside of itself. He simply distances himself more and more from any philosophy – Cartesian or Husserlian – that attempts to found its source on an absolute ground without any presupposition.

Endnotes

1. *Fallible Man* was originally translated into English in 1965. A revised translation by the same translator was issued in 1986. This section of *On Ricoeur* follows the earlier, 1965, edition.

3
From Symbol
to Text

In *The Symbolism of Evil*, Ricoeur showed how "the fault" and the human experience of suffering and anxiety found expression in symbols and myths of various kinds. Symbols, he argued, were double-meaning expressions that possessed "an inexhaustible-depth" (CI 290). In the absence of knowing rationally what ultimately such symbols signify, symbols nonetheless do give rise to thought through interpretation. This led to the larger question of the relationship between symbols and philosophical reflection. It is not readily apparent how the interpretation of symbols could give rise to existential concepts and add to our reflection on existence.

Ricoeur does not solve this dilemma immediately yet envisages the need to move from a hermeneutics of symbols to a more general hermeneutics, one that would treat all sign systems objectively. Ricoeur's redefinition of philosophical reflection as hermeneutics is inaugurated in *Freud and Philosophy: An Essay in Hermeneutics* (1965) and *The Conflict of Interpretations* (1969). It would be misleading to suggest that Ricoeur foresaw his way through this shift of emphasis easily. The period after *The Symbolism of Evil* coincided with a change of paradigms in French philosophy where a preoccupation with post-Husserlian phenomenologies and existentialism was replaced with a growing fascination in the various expressions of structuralist arguments. The rise of structuralism posed certain challenges. In choosing to respond to such challenges Ricoeur's development of a general hermeneutics would be punctuated and accentuated by a set of external polemics and internal wars that would last almost twenty years (PR 17).

Freud

Ricoeur's detour through psychoanalysis is not unlikely given Freud's concern with guilt and the need for an interpretative understanding of symbolic figures. More specifically, in reading Freud, Ricoeur wants to make good on his wager that symbols can lead to a concrete reflection on existence. But the mediation between symbols and reflection is not a direct one. It must be constructed within language. The pre-eminent model for this construction is psychoanalysis and its interpretation of dreams. "By making dreams not only the first object of his investigation, but a model ... of all the disguised, substitutive, and fictive expressions of human wishing or desire, Freud invites us to look to dreams themselves for the various relations between desire and language" (FP 5). Dreams are symbolic expressions that bring the primitive experience of desire to light. Psychoanalysis is a space where these symbolic expressions and interpretation confront one another. Ricoeur will call this space of confrontation "the hermeneutic field" (FP 8). It is only here, in the hermeneutic field, where the problem of symbolism becomes coextensive with the problem of language and where the possibility of recovering meaning exists.

There are two lessons to be garnered from placing the dream-text in the hermeneutic field. First, psychoanalysis quickly reveals how consciousness is not the place and origin of meaning. In light of the unconscious, psychoanalysis shows quite distinctly that consciousness cannot totalize itself – it cannot be its own ground. It shows that immediate consciousness is not necessarily genuine consciousness and that the human subject is actually dispossessed from itself as it appears to itself in the form of consciousness. This dispossession is necessary for the regressive path back to the source of meaning in desire, a source that exists prior to the division between subject and object. While Ricoeur depicts this de-centering of consciousness as a wound upon the *cogito* and a humiliation to the subject of reflection, it nonetheless underscores the long route to meaning that must be endured if symbols are to be taken seriously as ciphers of meaning not self-evident to consciousness.

Second, symbols can be interpreted in different manners given different frames of reference. This is no better displayed than in how psychoanalysis and the phenomenology of religion come to diametrically opposed responses to the efficacy of symbols. Both forms of analysis displace consciousness as the home of meaning and each "embraces the whole of man and each claims to interpret and understand the totality of man's being" (CI 320). While the phenomenology of religion has as its intended object the "sacred" and the understanding of Being as "truth" through its analysis of ritual action and mythical speech, psychoanalysis will pursue its own truth of the same symbols as merely being functional to the economy of instincts. For Freud nothing sacred is to be found. We invent gods to exorcise fear, to reconcile us to the cruelty of fate and to assuage the incurable malaise caused by the death instinct. Strikingly evident in this example is how the density of meaning in symbolic expressions permits a surplus of meaning and encourages a conflict of possible interpretations. Ricoeur's question is whether or not such a conflict of interpretations can bring us to a concrete reflection on existence. In this initial outline of the problem however he quite readily admits: "There is no general hermeneutics, no universal canon for exegesis, but only disparate and opposed theories concerning the rules of interpretation. The hermeneutical field ... is internally at variance with itself" (FP 26). Ricoeur will eventually work toward a position whose aim is not to resolve such conflicts but to work with them and to make them productive.

Given this background it may be instructive to list some of the more salient points Ricoeur emphasizes in this magnificent text. It should be kept in mind that *Freud and Philosophy* "broke free of its initial motivation" to provide a sequel to *The Symbolism of Evil* in that it no longer sought to provide a restorative reading of the myths of culpability (PR 191).

1) *Symbols and Language.* In the opening pages of *Freud and Philosophy*, Ricoeur suggests that dreams cloak our desires such that we "go forth in disguise." The disguise is the ruse of a symbol's double meaning. The problem of double meaning is not peculiar to the analysis of dreams. It is from the phenomenology of religion, for example, that we learn how the great cosmic symbols of earth, water, life, trees and stones – along with the mythical narratives describing the beginning and the end of things – are the first means by which human beings place themselves in relation to reality (FP 7). In the meantime, symbols are not some odd and esoteric set of ciphers belonging to an impenetrable realm. Symbols belong to human beings and, as such, do not stand apart from language. Whether one looks at the cosmic symbols brought to light by the phenomenology of religion, the dream

symbolism revealed by psychoanalysis, or the creations of the poet, symbols form a totality that find their expression in language.

> There is no symbolism prior to man who speaks, even though the power of symbols is rooted more deeply, in the expressiveness of the cosmos, in what desire wants to say, in the varied image contents that men have. But in each case it is in language that the cosmos, desire, and the imaginary achieve speech (FP 16).

Symbols are not a non-language. Far from falling outside the bounds of language, symbols raise the experience of the world to articulation. More crucial is that every *mythos* involves a latent *logos* demanding to be expressed. "This is why there are no symbols without the beginning of interpretation; where one man dreams, prophesies, or poetizes, another rises up to interpret. Interpretation organically belongs to symbolic thought and its double meaning" (FP 19).

2) *The Concept of Interpretation*. While interpretation is the route through which the problem of symbols enters into the wider problem of language, interpretation itself is problematic. What does it mean exactly to interpret? While the science of interpretation has been commonly referred to as hermeneutics, historically its application has lacked a consistent program. Where Aristotle originally saw interpretation as a study of words in hope of reducing them to an univocal state of meaning in order to say something of something, hermeneutics is more commonly associated with biblical exegesis (FP 20ff). Traditionally, biblical exegetes dealt solely with the written word. They applied four levels of meaning to biblical texts – the literal, the allegorical, the analogical and the symbolic. Their aim was to overcome the distance of historical and cultural reinterpretations in hopes of understanding the original divine intention behind Holy Scripture.

Another form of hermeneutics not covered in *Freud and Philosophy* but of great importance to Ricoeur is the late nineteenth century thought of Friedrich Schleiermacher (1768-1834) and Wilhelm Dilthey (1833-1911). While it was Dilthey specifically who distinguished *understanding* in the human sciences from *explanation* in the natural sciences, both thinkers succumbed to a romantic form of hermeneutics where interpretation meant transcending the horizons of the interpreter's historical situation in order to recapture the author's original subjectivity (HS 45ff).

A more contemporary version of hermeneutics belongs to the phenomenology of religion in its attempt to recover the intended object (the sacred) in ritual, myth and belief. Such a hermeneutics aims at a "restoration of a meaning addressed to me in the manner of a message, a proclamation, or ... kerygma" (CI 27).

Ricoeur identifies another current of hermeneutics that not only contests the existence of such an object of religion, but pursues an destructive critique that tears off masks and undermines all forms of false meaning. Ricoeur calls this stream of hermeneutics "the school of suspicion" and identifies Karl Marx (1818-1883), Friedrich Nietzsche (1844-1900) and Sigmund Freud (1856-1939) as the three masters of suspicion (FP 32). For these three thinkers the *real* significance of things is never in the *apparent* and the immediate but always stands elsewhere, beneath the surface. For Marx, the truth of consciousness was connected to the economic modes of production; for Nietzsche, it was connected to the will to power; and, for Freud, it was connected to the unconscious. While Ricoeur recognizes all three for "clearing the horizon for a more authentic word, for a new reign of Truth ... by the invention of an art of interpreting," their real contribution was showing how sources of signification may exist yet are removed from the immediate grasp of consciousness. Each thinker helped to show, albeit in a different manner, immediate consciousness *per se* to be a false consciousness (FP 33; CI 18). Meaning is not directly available to consciousness. It is not reducible to the immediate consciousness of meaning. The masters of suspicion displaced immediate consciousness as the origin of meaning and shifted it elsewhere such that meaning must be recovered and restored by deciphering the expressions of consciousness. "The man of suspicion carries out in reverse the work of falsification of the man of guile" (FP 34). Yet for all their interpretative ingenuity the final word on interpretation does not rest with them. Beyond recognizing the need for a destructive critique they did not explain "what thought, reason, and even faith still mean" (CI 248). Each of their stratagems tends toward a narrowing of the existential field to a particular theme (economics, will-to-power, psychism) that fails to consider "the grace of imagination [and] the upsurge of the possible" (FP 36).

3) *Archeology and Teleology of the Subject*. Up to this point, Ricoeur has shown that symbols have something to offer philosophy – the spur to see understanding more in terms of interpretation. The real problem now is not simply why interpretation, but how can philosophical reflection depend upon pre-constituted forms of hermeneutics that seem at times mutually exclusive. "To justify the

recourse to symbols in philosophy is ultimately to justify ... the war of hermeneutics within itself" (FP 42). While Ricoeur will not solve this particular problem in *Freud and Philosophy* the rest of the work will be devoted to revealing – via the works of Freud – to what degree philosophical reflection is ultimately dependent on interpretation and why, in one way or another, it must eventually become hermeneutic.

Philosophical reflection always begins with positing the self as a first truth. "Since this truth cannot be verified like a fact, nor deduced like a conclusion, it has to posit itself in reflection; its self-positing is reflection" (FP 43). But this first act of reflection doesn't really count as self-knowledge if we assume it arises from itself like the Cartesian *cogito* (I am, I think) and grasps itself directly in the experience of doubt. Such a self-positing "truth is as vain as it is invincible" since the ego is never given in any psychological evidence or pure intellectual intuition (FP 43; CI 17). Reflection is not intuition. As already mentioned, immediate consciousness always tends to be a false consciousness.

What is important in terms of self-knowledge is not simply the epistemological status of a fact that we ourselves posit in the first place – the "I am." What claims a philosophical reflection can make about self-knowledge must first be chastised by the acknowledgement that our original effort to be and to exist is not transparent to ourselves. It must be recovered. Evoking the thought of Nabert, Ricoeur sees reflection as an "*appropriation of our effort to exist and of desire to be, through the works which bear witness to that effort and desire*" (FP 46). The notion of appropriation acknowledges that the original situation from which reflection proceeds is "forgetfulness." It recognizes the fact that "I am lost ... among the objects of the world, separated from the center of my existence ... [and] that I do not first possess what I am. ... That is why reflection is a task ... the task of making my concrete experience equal to the positing 'I am'" (FP 45; CI 329). Henceforth, reflection and consciousness will no longer coincide and reflection should not be confused with any type of immediate intuition of meaning. Such intuition is impotent to either penetrate the vain and empty abstraction of the "I am, I think" or fully appreciate our effort to exist. If the positing of the self is no longer a given then it must endure the task of recovering itself by deciphering its own signs lost in the world of culture.

> The ultimate root of our problem lies in this primitive connection between the act of existing and the signs we deploy

in our works; reflection must become interpretation because I cannot grasp the act of existing except in signs scattered in the world. This is why a reflective philosophy must include the results, methods, and presuppositions of all the sciences that try to decipher and interpret the signs of man (FP 46).

Ricoeur's turn to Freud becomes clearer on this point. Whenever Freud speaks of instincts and desire, he speaks of them from the level of expression, that is, in and from certain effects of meaning which lend themselves to interpretation and can be treated as texts – dreams texts or symptomatic texts that find expression in the order of language. In bringing the experience of desire to language, it is brought into the totality of human experience which philosophy undertakes to reflect upon and to understand (CI 164).

A dream does not speak the language of consciousness as a play of meanings. Dreams are a mixed discourse (FP 65ff). The dream-text is a mixture of meaning and desire where dreams are the end result of desire's effect upon meaning. In other terms, dream symbolism is the milieu of expression where desire is uttered. Ricoeur proposed "the semantics of desire" to designate this interweaving of two kinds of relations: relations of force, expressed in dynamics (drive, cathexis, condensation, displacement, repression, return of the repressed, and so on) and relations of meaning, expressed in an exegesis of meaning (thought, wish, intelligibility, disguise, interpretation, interpolations, and so on) (PR 20). Symbolism occurs because what is symbolized is found initially in a nonlinguistic reality that Freud termed instinct. "That which, in the unconscious, is capable of speaking, that which is able to be represented, refers back to a substrate that cannot be symbolized: desire as desire" (FP 454). The only access to this primordial desire is through its psychic representations that are neither biological nor semantic. It is these emissaries and their derivatives that are both revealed and hidden in the meaning interpreted from symptoms, dreams, myths, ideals and illusions. "Far from moving in closed linguistic circle, we are ceaselessly at the juncture of the erotic and the semantic. The power of the symbol is due to the fact that double meaning is the mode in which the very ruse of desire is expressed" (CI 66).

This semantics of desire only confirms that the home of meaning is not to be sought in consciousness but elsewhere. This "elsewhere" must be recaptured by an interpretative process – a process that will never attain the instincts but only their psychic representatives (FP 435).

Ricoeur calls this backward movement of psychoanalysis toward the subject of desire "the archaeology of the subject." The end-point of such movement is not the self-constituting subject but a wounded Cogito, one "that posits itself but does not possess itself; a Cogito that sees its original truth only in and through the avowal of the inadequacy, illusion, and lying of actual consciousness" (FP 439). This fractured Cogito owes it wounded sense to what grounds its existence – the desire and effort to be. Desire is the indestructible and irretrievable archaism that accompanies such exteriorizations as dreams. In following these various expressions back we are led to a beginning but a beginning that that can never be made transparent.

Freud's regressive movement oriented toward the archaic is only part of a larger, conceivable dialectic that includes a progressive movement of "becoming conscious." In order for the subject to attain its true being, it is not enough for it to discover the inadequacy of its self-awareness. Another humiliation is yet in store. The subject must also discover that the process of becoming conscious, through which it appropriates the meaning of its existence as desire and effort, does not belong to it. Guided by Hegel's *Phenomenology of the Spirit*, Ricoeur argues that the subject must mediate self-consciousness through spirit or mind, that is, through the figures that give a *telos* to this "becoming conscious" (FP 459). Meaning for Hegel resides in the spirit. The spirit is the dialectic of the cultural figures that mediate the meaning and process of self-consciousness. In this sense consciousness is a movement, the movement of meaning, but it does not contain in itself the impetus of such a movement. In capturing the spirit that dwells in this movement, consciousness internalizes the movement but not its source (FP 463). It is a movement that must be rediscovered in the objective structure of institutions, monuments, works of art and culture which are also symbolic.

Ricoeur argues that both the regressive archeology of reflection and this progressive genesis of meaning are parts of one dialectic that symbols coordinate in a concrete unity. In sharing the same source – desire – regression and progression do not represent two opposing processes but are the abstract terms designating the two end limits of a single scale of symbolization. This regressive-progressive dialectic demands two hermeneutics developing in opposite directions: one that is turned toward the revival of archaic meanings belonging to the infancy of humankind and the other toward the emergence of figures that anticipate our spiritual adventure.

Ricoeur exemplifies the unity between the two hermeneutics – the regressive (archeological) and the progressive (teleological) – in showing the overdetermination of meaning in Sophocles' myth of *Oedipus Rex*, a "tragedy ... built around a fantasy well known to the interpretation of dreams, the fantasy in which we live through the childhood drama that we call oedipal" (FP 515). On the one hand, in clinical psychoanalysis, the myth becomes a complex and is carried back in analysis to the archaic background of infancy; on the other hand, there is the drama of coming to self-consciousness and self-recognition which is a search for truthfulness (FP 518). "For Sophocles, the problem is not that Oedipus killed his father and married his mother but that he denied that he was the man, so that it's a tragedy of truth" (RI 460). In short, *Oedipus Rex* is a prime example of how regression and progression can be carried by the same symbol. This conflict of interpretation arises because dreams and works of art are psychical expressions of the same nature. Their unity is assured by the fact that they share "the same 'matter' of desire" but are distinguished by what Freud called the diversion of aims or sublimation. Within their intentional structure symbols are a union of desire and multiple aims or intentions with emphasis upon either disguising this primordial desire or upon the disclosure of a further, spiritual meaning (FP 521).

4) Conclusions. While it might be argued that the entire point of *Freud and Philosophy* has been to undermine psychoanalysis' claim to be an observational science and to recast it as a hermeneutic discipline, this would miss the point. What Ricoeur has hoped to offer was not a better understanding of Freud but of self-understanding. The entire exercise has been one of concrete reflection (FP 493), that is, of bringing what is so close to us, yet so hidden in symbol, closer to language through interpretation. Ricoeur's excursus through psychoanalysis has shown that

> the appropriation of my desire to exist is impossible by the short path of consciousness; only the long path of interpretation of signs is open. Such is my working hypothesis in philosophy. I call it *concrete reflection*, that is, *the cogito mediated by the entire universe of signs* (CI 264-5).

Psychoanalysis as a hermeneutic discipline assists reflective philosophy to emerge from abstraction. It has shown quite convincingly that understanding the world of signs and symbols is a means of understanding oneself and that the symbolic universe is the milieu and medium toward self-explanation. It is only in a hermeneutic field, like psychoanalysis, where symbol and interpretation are brought together in the fullness of language that we might learn *to think better* in accord with symbols. In bringing symbols to the fullness of language through interpretation, philosophical reflection continues its attempt to understand existence and meaning. It is an understanding however that is now thoroughly hermeneutic. "The rootedness of reflection in life is itself understood in reflective consciousness only in the form of a hermeneutic truth" (FP 458). In this period of his methodological development Ricoeur will generally recognize hermeneutics as "any discipline which proceeds by interpretation" where hidden meaning is discerned in apparent meaning. The task of hermeneutics is not exclusive to psychoanalysis but reflective of such diverse disciplines as "the semantics of linguists, ... the phenomenology and comparative history of religions, literary criticism, etc."(CI 264).

Language as Discourse

Although the importance of language was recognized in his works on the symbols of evil and Freud, it remained a peripheral topic until Ricoeur decided to confront structuralism in the early 1960s. While the move from Freud to structuralism might seem haphazard, Ricoeur recognized that both the structuralist critique originating from linguistics and the psychoanalytic critique originating from Freud called into question the primacy of the speaking subject. Ricoeur called this convergence the "semiological challenge" and his response to it sets into motion the final drive toward a definition of hermeneutics based on the model of the text (HS 35; CI 236). This challenge is elaborated in several articles but more concisely in a set of lectures entitled *Interpretation Theory: Discourse and the Surplus of Meaning* (1976).

Structuralism encompasses a variety of positions associated with such names as Barthes, Levi-Strauss and Althusser. What unites them is an underlying linguistic model whose origin is traceable to the Swiss linguist Ferdinand de Saussure who wrote in the early part of the last century. To Ricoeur's liking the presuppositions of Saussure's system of linguistics found a more contemporary formulation in Louis Hjelmslev's (1899-1965) *Prolegommena to a Theory of Language*. It is on the basis of this work that Ricoeur pursues his interrogation of structuralism.

There are several key presuppositions to the linguistic – semiotic – model that underpins structuralism (CI 81; IT 3). First, structural linguistics distinguishes between language (*la langue*) and speech (*la parole*). Language (*la langue*) is understood as a set of signs and codes that underlie and structure our linguistic practices. Such signs can be isolated and studied as homogeneous objects of science. Speech is more dispersed and involves individual performance and psychophysiological execution. Owing to it heterogeneous and contingent nature speech is not easily open for structural analysis and therefore it is of lesser importance than language. Second, where speech incorporates change over time and is considered diachronic, language (*la langue)* is atemporal or synchronic. Structural linguistics subordinates diachrony in favor of the synchronic. Third, in a system of language there are no absolute terms but only relations of mutual dependence. This means that meanings attached to isolated signs are not important. Language is a system of signs defined by their differences alone. Fourth, structural linguistics treats the collection of signs as a closed and autonomous system of internal dependencies. It is a closed system of signs existing only for itself. Any reference to reality is blocked by the imprisonment of the sign within the confines of the system. As self-contained system language (*la langue*) no longer appears as a mediation between minds and things - it no longer mediates reality.

This model of synchronic linguistics becomes problematic when applied to other dimensions of existence where structure can be detected such as in myths, rituals, architecture, social etiquette and economic exchange. Such a move presupposes that all realms of life are structured in a homologous manner to the laws of the sign. In Lévi-Strauss' structural anthropology, for example, the model is applied to the analysis of myths. The result is that the story of the narrative sequence is regarded as merely a surface that covers a more important depth-structure (CI 34ff). Mythic texts operate, he claims, based on codes or units similar to semiotic units. These units or "mythemes" can be treated much like linguistic units in that they are neither sonorous nor carry a message; they are simply oppositive differences or inter-plays of relationships (FT 112ff). A myth's meaning is not found in the message but in its arrangement of mythemes. As such, narrative content is completely sacrificed to a code and the search for meaning is subordinated to the search for structure.

Ricoeur sees several problems with this model in general (CI 83ff).

First, it excludes the "opening-out of language," that is, the capacity of language to say something about something to someone (CI 96). This inherent capacity is not rooted in some atemporal structure of linguistic relations but in the very being of the speaking subject. At the heart of spoken language is an "ontological vehemence" that keeps language from closing in on itself and demands that it give testimony to the ontological dimension of human experience (RM 299; FT 20). More, the linguistic-semiotic model just described cannot account for the creation of meaning and free creation of new expressions. The act of speaking is an individual performance that cannot be explained solely on the bases of synchronic structures. If one took seriously the structuralist presupposition that the laws of the sign apply equally to the larger units of language like the sentence, the poem and narratives, then meaning would be completely imprisoned within the sign. This would make the subject's search for meaning superfluous. In Lévi-Strauss' objective explanation of myths, for example, a myth is reduced to a "logical operation" (FT 120). What such an explanation lacks is understanding, or more specifically, existential understanding in that a myth points towards "limit situations, toward the origin and the end, toward death, suffering, and sexuality" (FT 121). To eliminate these conflicts of existence provoked by myths reduces "the theory of myth to the necrology of the meaningless discourses of mankind" (FT 164). Lastly, the structuralist model excludes history. It does not take into account that history is a complicated process whereby human beings produce themselves and produce culture through the use and production of language.

While Ricoeur agrees that structural analyses of various kinds offer novel and fruitful types of explanations, structuralism can never establish itself as a philosophy. Its real danger lies in placing the source of meaning and signification "in a different field from that of the intentional aimings of the subject" (CI 250). For the structural linguist the order of the system precedes the speaking subject. This sets the meaning of the structure prior to the meaning of the subject. In short, the subject and its effort to be and to exist become irrelevant and insignificant. In order to redress this "semiological challenge" to the primacy of the subject and the creation of meaning Ricoeur chooses to re-examine the basic distinctions between language-as-system (*la langue*) and speech (*la parole*) by emphasizing the role of discourse over system.

Ricoeur agrees that language can be articulated on many levels with regard to internal and oppositive relations (e.g.: the phoneme, the morpheme, the lexeme, etc.). Yet there is a discontinuity once language is spoken as speech. The very reason why speech (*la parole*) was marginalized in the above model was that it was individual, historical, contingent and heterogeneous. It could not be systematized into a play of opposites between discrete entities and therefore it could not be made into an object of science. To Ricoeur's mind this resistance to systematization is not a weakness in spoken speech but its strength. Spoken speech, which Ricoeur will specifically refer to as *discourse*, is a synthetic construction irreducible to an analytic combination of sign units. By discourse Ricoeur does not mean all the aspects of language inferred by linguist "but the messages which we produce freely on the foundation and the structure of language" (RI 442). He will also sometimes generally refer to discourse as the "acts of language equal to or greater than the sentence" (TN1 ix).

Four traits of discourse are of note. First, following Emile Benvéniste's (1902-1976) theory of discourse, language has two functions: the semiotic function based on the unit of the sign and the semantic function based on the unit of the sentence. Where semiotic signs are atemporal and must always remain virtual in speaking, the sentence is realized temporally. A sentence is an instance of discourse (HS 198). It is the actual *event* of speaking. Moreover there is no way of passing from the word as a lexical sign to the sentence by mere extension of a structural methodology. The sentence is not a larger or more complex word. It is a new entity. A sentence may be broken into words but the words are something other than short sentences. A sentence is made up of signs but is not itself a sign (IT 7). This opposition of system and event has an important consequence. Where the system of language is always a finite and fixed set of phonetic or lexical signs, discourse exhibits creation and innovation. It is in the combination of words that new constellations of meanings appear.

A second trait of discourse is that it implies the presence of a subject. Discourse refers back from itself to its own speaker by a complex set of indicators such as personal pronouns. In language as system there is no subject because the personal pronoun is an empty sign. However, in the event of speaking, in discourse, there is always an "I" that speaks. This "I" is not a concept but a living word. The signification of the "I" is singular in each instance; by uttering it, I anchor myself in the here and now of my own situation (CI 255). In short, the instance of discourse is self-referential.

Another important trait about discourse is that it is always about something. Words are turned from the inert world of the system to an actual world. An uttered sentence refers to a world that it claims to describe, to express or to represent. It is in discourse that the symbolic function of language is fully actualized.

Last, an instance of discourse is the instance of dialogue. Discourse not only has a world but an another person, an interlocutor to whom something is addressed (HS 198). The act of speech appears as a way of trespassing or overcoming the fundamental solitude of each human being such that some small aspect of our individual lived experience might be communicated (IT 15).

These traits hope to re-establish language and speaking as openness, that is, to show that language as discourse is, at least in principle, an open and unlimited process of creation of meaning.

Ricoeur elaborates on the features of discourse with regard to an internal dialectic between event and meaning. Discourse is an event in the world that actualizes language and gives it existence. While such an event might be conceived as being transitory and fleeting, the event of discourse does not pass into oblivion because it can be repeated and recognized as the same insofar as it carries meaning. This meaning arises not so much as a function of the words employed but by the fact that the event of discourse penetrates beyond language – beyond the closed world of signs – and mediates reality or the extra-linguistic world. In discussing the notion of meaning Ricoeur borrows much from English experts in philosophical semantics but draws more consistently upon Gottlob Frege's (1848-1925) two objective aspects of meaning. A sentence for Frege has an ideal sense (what is said) and a real reference (about what it is said) (IT 19). Only the sentence level allows us to distinguish "what is said" and "about what it is said." The sense is the ideal object which the proposition intends and is purely immanent in discourse. The reference is the truth-value of the proposition that reaches toward reality. Reference thus distinguishes discourse from language (*la langue*). Language-as-system has no creative relation to reality because its signs and words brings meaning back onto itself. "Only discourse ... intends things, applies itself to reality, [and] expresses the world" (HS 140).

The dialectic of sense and reference is significant for Ricoeur because reference in discourse says something not only about things but about the ontological condition of our being in the world. "Language is not a world of its own. It is not even a world. But because we are in the world, because we are affected by situations, and because we orient ourselves in those situations, we have something to say, we have experience to bring to language" (IT 20-1). Language begins not with structure or a system of oppositive signs but with a "more originary move starting from the experience of being in the world and proceeding from this ontological condition towards its expression in language" (IT 21). The foundations of linguistics lie, therefore, in discourse's dialectic of sense and reference. It is this dialectic that gives credit to the fact that language must begin with the speaking subject and not within its own inert systems of combinatory signs.

The concept of discourse as the event of meaning, of sense and of reference, becomes the starting point of two further investigations. One inquiry will go in the direction of units larger than sentences, to a theory of the written *text* and its interpretation. Another will deal with units smaller than the sentence, the *word*, and deal with a word's polysemic, metaphorical and symbolic qualities. The latter will be dealt with in the chapter to follow with respect to imagination.

World of the Text

Ricoeur begins to unfurl the hermeneutical implications of discourse by talking in terms of texts. While a text can be defined as any discourse fixed in writing it is primarily a *work* of discourse. To say that a text is a work of discourse is to say that it is a structured totality that cannot be decomposed merely into the sentences that comprise it. Such a totality arises in light of the rules that define its literary genre and transform the discourse into a poem, a play or a novel. The idea that a genre can be imposed on discourse is important because it means that language takes on a form and becomes a material that can be worked upon. As a work it enables "structural methods to be applied to discourse itself" and permits a process of interpretation to begin in earnest. "Hermeneutics ... remains the art of discerning the discourse in the work; but this discourse is only given in and through the structures of the work" (HS 138).

As noted, not only is the text a work of discourse but it is also something fixed in writing. While speaking and writing are legitimate modes of discourse's realization, writing subjects discourse to a set of characteristics which detach the text from the conditions of the spoken word. These characteristics are described in terms of "distanciation"

50

(HS 131ff). Writing, for example, permits the "matter" of the text to escape from the finite intentional horizon of its author and transcend the psycho-sociological conditions of its own production. Similarly, a written text detaches itself from the dialogical situation with regard to the original audience. It becomes addressed to an unknown reader and potentially to whoever knows how to read. The fate of every text is that it becomes "decontextualized" from its original social and historical conditions of productions.

There is one last form of distanciation that is perhaps the most important. In writing, the here and now of two speakers is abolished and the concrete conditions of pointing to what their discourse refers no longer exists. Ricoeur calls this the "abolition of ostensive reference" (HS 141). The emancipation of the text from the oral situation entails a veritable upheaval in the relations between language and the world. In virtue of this loss of ostensive reference each text is free to enter into relation with all the other texts that come to take the place of the circumstantial reality referred to by living speech. This relation of the text to text and the effacement of the world about which we speak opens up "the quasi-world of the text" or literature.

> The eclipse of the circumstantial world by the quasi-world of texts can be so complete that, in a civilization of writing, the world itself is no longer what can be shown in speaking but is reduced to a kind of 'aura' which written works unfold. Thus we speak of the Greek world or the Byzantine world. This world can be called 'imaginary', in the sense that it is *represented* by writing in lieu of the world *presented* by speech; but this imaginary world is itself a creation of literature. (HS 149)

The mistake, Ricoeur forewarns, would be to assume that the abolition of ostensive reference in fiction of all types (folktales, myths, novels and plays) entails that the text is without reference. This is not the case. The abolition of ostensive reference is not the abolition of all reference. "There is no discourse so fictional that it does not connect up with reality" (HS 141). This initial effacement of the first order or ostensive reference effected by writing (especially with regard to poetry and fiction) permits the freeing of a second order reference. This latter reference is the referent of all literature. It is no longer pertains to our situational reference to an actual world (*Umwelt*) but the non-situational reference to a symbolic world (*Welt*) projected by the non-ostensive references of every text that we have read, understood and loved. "The effacement of the ostensive and descriptive reference

51

liberates a power of reference to aspects of our being in the world that cannot be said in a direct descriptive way, but only alluded to, thanks to the referential values of metaphoric and, in general, symbolic expressions" (IT 37). The "world of the text" frees us from the visibility and limitation of situations by opening up a world where we can exercise new dimensions of our being (HS 202).

To explicate the purpose of a text revealing this new second order reference Ricoeur introduces the dialectic complement to distanciation called "appropriation." This term literally means "'make one's own' what was initially 'alien.'" It complements the aim of all hermeneutics in struggling against cultural distance and historical alienation. This can only be achieved by some act that "brings together, equalizes, renders contemporary and similar" (HS 185). For Ricoeur this act is appropriation. It signifies the activity whereby the present reader of a text does not seek to rejoin the original intentions of the author but to expand his or her conscious horizons by actualizing the meaning of the text. Appropriation is more than empathy with a text. It is understanding at and through distance; it means there is something of the text that is applicable to the present situation of the reader.

> What would we know of love and hate, of moral feelings and, in general, of all that we call the *self*, if these had not been brought to language and articulated by literature? Thus what seems most contrary to subjectivity, and what structural analysis discloses as the texture of the text, is the very *medium* within which we can understand ourselves (HS 143).

We understand ourselves because what we appropriate from texts is a proposed world. The proposed world is not behind the text like some hidden intention but in front of it, as something the work unfolds, reveals and discovers. "Henceforth, to understand is *to understand oneself in front of the text*" (HS 143). To be sure, the reader is not the one who projects him or herself. The reader is invited to follow "the 'arrow' of meaning and endeavors to 'think in accordance with' it, [and] engenders a new *self*-understanding" (HS 193).

Enough emphasis cannot be put on the function of reading and appropriation. "Reading is the *pharmakon*, the 'remedy,' by which the meaning of the text is 'rescued' from the estrangement of distanciation" effected by writing (IT 43). Reading is the concrete act in which the destiny of the text is fulfilled. Appropriation is not something arbitrary insofar as it is the recovery of that which is at work within the text. But what an interpreter reads is not only a re-saying of what the text is about but an activity that culminates in his or her own self-interpretation.

By 'appropriation,' I understand this: that the interpretation of a text culminates in the self-interpretation of a subject who thenceforth understands himself better, understands himself differently, or simply begins to understand himself. This culmination of the understanding of a text in self-understanding is characteristic of the kind of reflective philosophy which, on various occasions, I have called 'concrete reflection.' Here hermeneutics and reflective philosophy are correlative and reciprocal. ... Thus it must be said, ... that reflection is nothing without the mediation of signs and works, and that explanation is nothing if it is not incorporated as an intermediary stage in the process of self-understanding. In short, in hermeneutical reflection – or in reflective hermeneutics – the constitution of the *self* is contemporaneous with the constitution of *meaning* (HS 158).

It should be recalled that in his study on Freud, Ricoeur had already pointed out consciousness was not a given but a task, one that necessitated the need for concrete reflection by way of two hermeneutics – an archeological and teleological path. In both cases the origin of meaning was displaced outside of consciousness and had to be recovered by the interpretation of dream-texts and signs external to the *cogito*. This original gesture of concrete reflection is now extended with respect to texts and finds its locus in the reader through appropriation.

Texts and Hermeneutics

The radical implication of making hermeneutics and reflective philosophy reciprocal in the constitution of both self and meaning is that they can no longer be understood as the exclusive activity of the reflective philosopher. The question becomes an ontological one. Ricoeur will agree with Heidegger that understanding is no longer a mode of knowledge but a mode of being – that mode of being that exists through understanding. If understanding as interpretation becomes the primordial condition of our finite being-in-the-world, then hermeneutics becomes inextricably tied to the understanding of being. "The subject that interprets himself while interpreting signs is no longer the *cogito;* ... he is a being who discovers, by exegesis of his own life, that he is placed in being before he ... possesses himself. In this way hermeneutics would discover a manner of existing which would remain from start to finish a *being-interpreted*" (CI 11).

Ricoeur however will not follow Heidegger uncritically and markedly distinguishes his hermeneutics from that of the latter thinker. Heidegger demonstrated that behind the whole activity of human life, and seeking its points of orientation as a being-in-the-world, is a mysterious openness to Being which is inseparably connected to our finitude. It is an openness that provokes us to break through the illusions of our everyday sense of self-sufficiency. Heidegger, Ricoeur argues, took the "short route" to Being by confining his attention to a fundamental ontology of Being in general and subordinating historical knowledge to ontological understanding (CI 10). Heidegger's "ontology of understanding" breaks with any discussion of method and carries itself directly to the level of an ontology of finite being in order to recover understanding as a mode of being (CI 8). In this sense, Heidegger attempted to inspect human being directly and to give a description of existence too quickly. On the contrary, Ricoeur sees himself taking the "long route" such that, between birth and death, human understanding is obliged to canvass a range of hermeneutic fields (symbols, myth, language and so forth) in which meaning has become hidden, dispersed or deferred. This long route aspires to carry reflection to the level of ontology, but only by degree, and then only *approaches the limit* of Being. It does not attempt to assimilate it.

In terms of texts themselves, Ricoeur has canvassed two options for interpretation. He has suggested that it cannot be reduced just to *explaining* a text as something absolute and closed in on itself in terms of some abstract combinatory system as suggested by structuralism. As well, *understanding* a text has little to do with reconstituting the intentions of the author or uncovering something hidden behind the text. Hermeneutics must include both functions of explanation and understanding (FT 125ff). It must seek in the text itself, on the one hand, the internal dynamic that governs the structuring of the work and, on the other, the power of the work to project itself outside itself in the representation of a world that I could inhabit (FT 18). Explanation and understanding are therefore two complementary elements in a single interpretative process. While explaining brings out the structure of the text, to understand a text is to follow the existential possibilities that it lays out. In fact, explanation and interpretation as understanding should be situated along a unique *hermeneutical arc* that integrates the opposing attitudes of explanation and understanding within an overall conception of reading as the recovering of meaning.

> If ... we consider structural analysis as a stage ... between a naïve interpretation and a critical interpretation, between a surface interpretation and a depth interpretation, then it would be possible to locate explanation and understanding at different stages of a unique *hermeneutical arc*. It is this depth semantics that constitutes the genuine object of understanding and that requires affinity between the reader and the kind of things the text is *about*. But we must not be misled by the notion of personal affinity. The depth semantics of the text is not what the author intended to say, but what the text is about, that is, the non-ostensive reference of the text (FT 164).

In short, understanding is entirely mediated by the whole of explanatory procedures that precede it and accompany it. The counterpart of any personal appropriation is not something that can be felt. It is the dynamic meaning released by the explanation that was identified above with the reference of the text, that is, its power of disclosing a world. This disclosure is possible because of the general dialectic between explanation and understanding that underpins the hermeneutical arc. The dialectic gives rise to one of Ricoeur's important maxims: "To explain more is to understand better" (TN1 x).

This small incursion into discourse, texts and interpretation should indicate quite clearly how far Ricoeur has moved in his thinking from a hermeneutics of symbol toward a hermeneutics that embraces all phenomena of a textual order. Moreover, it should be obvious that hermeneutics does not pretend to place us either at the foundation of things or at the beginning or end. Hermeneutics situates us in the middle of a conversation that always *belongs* to a historical tradition where we already find ourselves in communication with institutions, social roles and collectivities (groups, classes, nations, cultural traditions, and so forth) (HS 108). The notion of "belonging" derides any pretension to absolute knowledge and radically confirms the finitude of our understanding. All understanding is finite understanding in as much as it is historical and finds itself always already planted in "'long' intersubjective relations ... sustained by historical traditions" (HS 108). Hermeneutics is the activity whereby we distance ourselves from this belonging – this participation in existence as historical – and signify it in order to subject it to explanation and thereby understand ourselves better.

In pursuing a general hermeneutics Ricoeur has not completely abandoned his phenomenological roots. He sees them both grafted on to one another to form a sort of hermeneutical phenomenology. There are several reasons for such a grafting. First, phenomenology is considered to be the unsurpassable presupposition of hermeneutics because for phenomenology every question concerning any being whatsoever is a question about the meaning of that being. It sees every act of consciousness as a form of intentionality directed outside of itself and turned toward meaning "before consciousness is *for itself"* in reflection (HS 115). The theme of intentionality (consciousness is a consciousness of ...) breaks up the Cartesian identification between consciousness and self-consciousness and defines itself by the objects it aims at as opposed to a solipsistic account of its own aiming. Meaning, in turn, is the most general presupposition of hermeneutics since all experience is in principle expressible in some form.

Hermeneutics comes back to phenomenology in another manner, through its recourse to distanciation which is a variant of phenomenological bracketing (*epoché*). Here, meaning is placed at a distance from the "lived experience" to which we adhere purely and simply. If phenomenology begins when we interrupt lived experience in order to signify it, hermeneutics begins similarly when we interrupt our *belonging* to a historical lived experience transmitted by tradition (written documents, works, institutions, and monuments which render present the historical past) in order to understand it better (HS 117).

Last, both hermeneutics and phenomenology acknowledge that the linguistic dimension of experience is always derivative not primary. Gadamer, for example, argued that our aesthetic and historical experience "comes to language" rather then being something language produces. The expressions of experience that come to language constitute, in Ricoeur's mind, the most important phenomenological presupposition of hermeneutics (HS 118).

4

Imagination:
Metaphor and Narrative

One of the central themes that would capture Ricoeur's attention for most of the 1970s was the problem of semantic imagination. By semantic imagination he does not mean mental representations. Imagination for Ricoeur is always a dimension of language. It is a rule-governed activity that schematizes semantic fields by "reviving former experiences, awakening dormant memories, [and] irrigating adjacent sensorial fields" (FT 173). It is in this immense field of semantic imagination that he distinguished two domains: first, the formation of poetic language in the wake of metaphoric expressions and, second, the formation of narrative language in the wake of structural linguistics applied to story telling. *The Rule of Metaphor* (1975) was the result of the first investigation and *Time and Narrative* (Vols. 1-3) (1983-5) was the result of the second. Both works contributed to an exploration of what Ricoeur called semantic innovation, the creation of meaning on the basis of three units of language: the word, the sentence and the text.

In the Introduction to *Time and Narrative*, Ricoeur states that both metaphorical utterance and narrative discourse belong to "one vast poetic sphere" (TN1 xi). He believes that in studying the creative capacity of language one discovers its ability to reveal various aspects of reality. "Language in the making celebrates reality in the making" (RI 462). The nature of the relations between language and reality and emergent meaning is encapsulated in the question of metaphor. Ricoeur often refers to metaphor as a poetic text in miniature (RM 243; HS 167). It is metaphor that facilitates an eruption of meaning in the wake of a mutual shattering between language and reality.

57

> My conclusion is that the strategy of discourse implied in metaphorical language is neither to improve communication nor to insure univocity in argumentation, but to shatter and to increase our sense of reality by shattering and increasing our language. ... With metaphor we experience the metamorphosis of both language and reality (RI 85).

Metaphor

Understanding creativity in language begins with a feature peculiar to words, namely, the problem of polysemy (RM 113ff; CI 68; RI 76). It deals with the fact that depending on contexts a word will have more than one meaning. In phrases such as "the leg of the chair" and "the last leg of the journey" the term "leg" does not refer primarily to the physiological limb called a leg. A one-to-one relationship does not exist between word and meaning as much as there is a range of meanings that accompany one word. In ordinary language possible but unintended meanings are screened out by the sentence and the context in which it is employed in the actual instance of discourse. Left unchecked, polysemy can lead to immense ambiguity and misunderstanding that threatens the very purpose of language to mediate our experience of the world. Ricoeur speaks of two strategies applied to the problem of polysemy.

First, the scientific use of language attempts to minimize the polysemic nature of words and enforces a type of one-word and one-sense uniformity in its terminology. The scientific use of language tends to reduce language to a form of instrumentality where we use it solely to communicate at the lowest level or to manipulate things and people (RI 75; 448). All plurivocity of meaning is derided in favor of univocal terms. The result is a type of "well-formed language" that is technical, proficient and unambiguous but at the same time insular and incapable of expressing a multitude of experiences that erupt between humans and the world, between ourselves and within oneself (RI 75; FT 2)

Poetry, on the other hand, thrives on the polysemic nature of words and strives to make words mean as much as they can and not as little as they can. It does not suppress the plurivocity of meaning but cultivates it in order to evoke from language its tireless capacity to express meaning. Poetry suspends the functionalistic use of ordinary language.

Its task is not to provide information about what we call empirical reality but, instead, proposes a "world." A poem challenges us to change our way of looking at things by evoking certain feelings that create or induce the projection of a new horizon of being that renovates our current horizon. Feelings are much more than effervescent emotion. They are a manner of situating oneself within the world. "Nothing is more ontological than feeling."[1] It is by means of feeling that we inhabit the world. A poem speaks of the world as that within which we live. It structures differently our manner of living because it feeds us existentially by giving articulation to values, goals and feelings that orient our lives. Where the scientific use of language would like to reduce language to merely inform us of "what is," poetry endlessly strives to point out "what could be."

In order to emphasize the creative use of polysemy in poetic language, Ricoeur turns his attention toward the role of metaphor. The aim of the introductory studies in *The Rule of Metaphor* is to counter the common view that metaphor is a deviant naming or substitution in naming where one word (the figurative) is substituted for another (the literal) on the basis of a perceived resemblance (RM Study 3). Such a substitution theory presumes that a metaphor is nothing more than an ornamental embellishment that can be translated back or reduced easily to a more literal form. If this were so, then there would be no creation of meaning, just a substitution of terms. The metaphor would be esteemed for its emotive power rather than its cognitive value. In contrast, Ricoeur will elaborate an "interaction theory" of metaphor that sees a metaphor's creative capacities as the result of a semantic interaction – tension – between a word and the sentence in which it appears. For this reason Ricoeur is more apt to speak of metaphorical statements and moves away from seeing a metaphor as nothing more than confusion between lexical entities. A metaphorical statement like Shakespeare's "time is a beggar" is absurd if we attempt to logically search for some form of resemblance between "time" and "begging." However, "time" and "beggar" undergo an alteration of meaning that results from their interaction embraced by the entire statement. Time becomes more than chronology and beggar signifies more than an importunate vagrant. Taken together the original absurdity is transformed into a statement that "over-signifies" a meaning beyond the reach of either term alone.

The production of a metaphor is the instantaneous creation of discourse that brings two previously distant ideas together and *creates* a resemblance between them. Thanks to the productive imagination which grasps similarities in differences, new connections forge a live metaphor.[2] Metaphor operates by abolishing the logical distance between heretofore distinct semantic fields in order to produce a semantic shock which, in its turn, sparks the novel meaning of a metaphor (FT 173). The result of the semantic shock is to "say" something while "seeing as." It draws out a new semantic pertinence from the ruins of the literal meaning (RM 230ff).

Taken as an instance of discourse the newly discovered similarity between the two terms is explained as an act of imagination and creativity. The appearance of the metaphor is not a resemblance waiting to be discovered but something invented. "To say that a new metaphor is not taken from anywhere is to recognize it for what it is, namely, a creation of language that comes to be at that moment, a *semantic innovation* without status in the language as something already established with respect to either a designation or connotation" (RM 98). As Ricoeur often remarks, "there are no live metaphors in a dictionary" (IT 52). They are rightly non-public and unheard-of expressions revealing the very art and act of "living speech." Thanks to living speech language is brought to its own limits revealing "its properly creative capacities."[3]

The importance of understanding metaphor as an instance of discourse is especially appreciated with regard to the question of reference (RM Study 7). Live metaphors tell us something more that we didn't know before. They yield new insights into reality and suggest new ways of orienting oneself in the world. Metaphors achieve this ability by breaking the relation between language and things. Freed from the constraints of mere description metaphor is able to re-describe reality (RM 240ff). Metaphors have the uncanny ability to go beyond the world understood strictly as the totality of things and processes, causes and effects. Live metaphors coax us to see and to feel the world "as." They go a long way to enlarging the concept of "truth" such that "we cease to identify reality with empirical reality or, what amounts to the same thing, that we cease to identify experience with empirical experience" (FT 11). The sense of the real is no longer reducible to asking for the facts of what is empirically verifiable. To the degree that metaphors shatter and increase our capacity to speak about things in a novel manner, our sense of reality is also shattered and increased. A study of metaphor re-acquaints us with the creative capacity of language. In recovering this capacity of language to create and re-create, we discover reality itself in the process of being created. "When language is itself in the process of becoming once more potential it is attuned to this dimension of reality which itself is unfinished and in the making" (RI 462).

This brings Ricoeur to the thorny question of what exactly is the real (RM 246). If reality can be redescribed what is to count as "the real" and as "the truth?" Ricoeur addresses this question by reminding his readers that the real "'place' of metaphor, its most intimate and ultimate abode, is … the copula of the verb *to be*" (RM 7; 247). The power of metaphors is not restricted to permitting us to "seeing-as" but on a deeper ontological level it is the revealer of a "being-as." Metaphors move us from the saying what things literally "are" to what things are "like." In doing so metaphor states the "is" and "is not" at the same time. Recalling the example above, "time as a beggar" teaches us to see *as*, to see time like a beggar. On the surface we can see that the statement is literally false ("is not") but not untrue in permitting us to look at the experience of time in a new way ("is") (RM 255). Hence, metaphors imply not only a tensive use of language but also a tensive concept of reality (IT 68). In the interplay between differences and resemblances within metaphorical utterances we are asked to suspend the first order affects of ordinary language to the benefit of a second order reference. "It is precisely from this tensive apprehension that a new vision of reality springs forth, which ordinary vision resists because it is attached to the ordinary use of words. The eclipse of the objective, manipulable world thus makes way for the revelation of a new dimension of reality and truth" (IT 68).

Metaphors open doors to a world that is deeper than the empirical world where "being" is strictly a function of the here and now. They bring to language deeply rooted experiences that neither ordinary nor scientific language could approach. Ricoeur suggests that metaphorical language reveals the profound structures of human desire and its rootedness in the Earth. Metaphor, as a gift of discourse, comes to structure within language "the mythico-poetic depths" of human being.[4]

Does this mean that poetry and metaphor become Ricoeur's Promised Land of meaning and significance for human beings? Does this imply that hermeneutics becomes subordinate to poetry and that the search for meaning resides more in literature than in philosophy? Can philosophy be instructed by metaphor? Ricoeur details his response to such questions in the last study of *The Rule of Metaphor*. Philosophical discourse and poetic discourse are seemingly "heterogeneous." Where metaphor cannot easily be translated into a conceptual discourse like philosophy without losing its particular tensive quality, philosophical discourse cannot become quasi-poetical without blurring the need for conceptual clarity. But concepts do not arise automatically from either perception or images alone. They too are a creature of language. This is evidenced in the whole question of analogy (RM 259ff). Concepts are derived from inscriptions laid out when meanings draw away from a more fundamental metaphorical process inherent to discourse, that is, "the conceptual order is able to free itself from the play of double meaning and hence from the semantic dynamism characteristic of the metaphorical order" (RM 302). What seems on the surface to be a sharp disparity between the speculative and the poetic is actually a type of "interplay" arbitrated by interpretation. In fact interpretation is itself a mode of discourse that functions at the intersection of two domains, namely, the speculative and the metaphorical.

> On the one side, interpretation seeks the clarity of the concept; on the other, it hopes to preserve the dynamism of meaning that the concept holds and pins down. ... Metaphor is living not only to the extent that it vivifies a constituted language. Metaphor is living by virtue of the fact that it introduces the spark of imagination into a 'thinking more' at the conceptual level. The struggle to 'think more,' guided by the 'vivifying principle,' is the 'soul' of interpretation (RM 303).

"Thinking more," therefore, is not solely the purview of speculative discourse. As symbol gives rise to thought so does metaphor. Where metaphor opens up the depth-structures of reality, speculative discourse prevents thought from being delivered uncritically to poetical truth alone. Speculative discourse cannot reach meaning directly or create meaning *ex nihilo*. It cannot dispense with its relationship with the rich resources of poetic discourse and metaphor to increase and augment the capacity of our language to mediate meaning. The relationship between the two discourses is one of interpretation. Metaphorical truth is not something projected by us as much as it opens up a wider dimension of reality to which our life belongs. Ricoeur's closing line to *The Rule of Metaphor* is emblematic of this dynamic. "What is given to thought in this way by the 'tensional' truth of poetry is the most primordial, most hidden dialectic – the dialectic that reigns between the experience of belonging as a whole and the power of distanciation that opens up the space of speculative thought" (RM 313).

Narrative and Time

Ricoeur has repeated numerous times that the multi-volume work, *Time and Narrative* (1983-5), should be considered a companion text to *The Rule of Metaphor* (1975). On first blush the link between metaphor and narrative may not be self-evident. But as previously mentioned both themes manifest the same basic phenomenon of semantic innovation produced entirely on the level of discourse. With metaphor the innovation lies in the producing of a new semantic pertinence by means of an impertinent attribution ("Time is a beggar). With narrative the semantic innovation lies in the inventing of another work of synthesis – the plot – where a temporal unity is created out of a diversity of goals, causes, characters and events. It is this synthesis of the heterogeneous that brings narrative close to metaphor. In both cases the semantic innovation has its source in the productive imagination – an imagination according to rules – that consists of schematizing the synthetic operation. It is under the auspices of the productive imagination that both metaphor and narrative are able to produce "new logical species by predicative assimilation, in spite of the resistance of our current categorizations of language" (TN1 x; FT 9). In focusing his attention on this "one vast poetic sphere" Ricoeur believes he is readily able to show how narrative and metaphor mediate the production of meaning. It is only by looking closely at both metaphor and narrative that "human creativity is to be discerned and to be circumscribed within forms that make it accessible to analysis" (FT 8).

Important to both metaphor and narrative is the question of reference. Where metaphorical redescription reigned "in the field of sensory, emotional, aesthetic, and axiological values," the synthetic action of narrative applies "to the sphere of human action ... and its temporal values." Ricoeur sees in our ability to formulate narrative plots "the privileged means by which we re-configure our confused, unformed, and at the limit mute temporal experience" (TN1 xi).[5] Up to this point, Ricoeur had never published anything on time outside of articles that dealt with the problematic of history. By his own admission, "I was able to write on time only once I had perceived a meaningful connection between 'narrative function' and 'the human experience of time'" (PR 39). Subsequently, the three volumes of *Time and Narrative* will address the question of meaning and creativity by the attending to the ancient philosophical conundrum of "what is time?"

How is narrativity, as the construction or deconstruction of paradigms of story-telling, a perpetual search for new ways of expressing human time, a production or creation of meaning? That is my question (RI 463).

In the course of his study Ricoeur will depend upon a legion of thinkers who have previously tackled the difficult topic of time including such notables as Augustine, Kant, Husserl and Heidegger. The central problem is that we cannot think time owing to time's ultimate aporia (TN3 261). This aporia refers to a bifurcation or gap between a phenomenology of time (mortal/subjective time) and cosmic time (scientific/objective time). The latter refers to the seemingly infinite age of the cosmos considered as an endless anonymous natural time (the time of astronomy and physics). Mortal time, on the other hand, is the average finite natural life span of human being. In comparison to the geological age of the earth and the calculated age of stars and the galaxy, mortal time is extremely short. The stark contrast between the two times is what defines us as being-towards-death. As mere mortals, it is being confronted by the impersonal face of cosmic time that has given rise to so many elegies and lamentations that sing of the contrast between the time that remains and we who are merely passing. "Would we speak of the shortness of life, if it did not stand out against the immensity of time?" (TN3 93). The existential crisis of time owes itself to the fact that no matter how cleverly we plummet the depths of mortal time phenomenologically, cosmic time stands apart and indifferent to such human cleverness. As human beings we cannot think time in order to master it. We cannot constitute time *per se* – we can only submit to its passage. "Thinking encounters this failure not only on the occasion of the enigma of evil but also when time, escaping our will to mastery, surges forth on the side of what, in one way or another, is the true master of meaning" (TN3 261).

Time's inscrutability is ameliorated somewhat by reference to history. History is a sort of fracture zone between mortal time and cosmic time where the production and overlapping of meaning seems to compensate for the epistemological break between the two times. Is it not history, Ricoeur queries, that can bridge the gap between our sense of Being-towards-death and the cosmic time that envelops us? (TN3 95). Is it not with history that the memory of the dead clashes with the investigation of institutions, structures and world-time that is stronger than death?

In concentrating on history Ricoeur sees historical time as a "third time" which reinscribes lived time (mortal time) on cosmic time through "procedures of connection," namely, the calendar, succession of generations, archives, documents and other such traces (TN3 99ff). Since it is within historical time that "the trace" makes its appearance, historical time becomes the space that calls for human discourse. It is one of the spaces where story telling, from the strict viewpoint of the narrative formation of discourse, makes its appearance. A trace passed on from generation to generation, documented and stored, summons us to address the past – to recount it. To recount the past is to begin to understand the narrative embodiment of our temporal experience.

Ricoeur's demand on narrative, however, does not restrict itself exclusively to historical narrative. The claim will be made that *both* fictive and historical narratives bring into relief the temporal character of human being. Whether historical or fictional, all narratives make sense of time. Consequently, Ricoeur intends to defend the thesis that "time becomes human to the extent that it is articulated through a narrative mode, and narrative attains its full meaning when it becomes a condition of temporal experience" (TN1 52).[6] The result is the recognition of "human time." This notion of time is a fragile mix where the representing of the past of history and the imaginative variations of fiction coalesce such that the aporetic nature of time is not solved but put to work in a creative manner.

Such a thesis invites us to see that every story told expresses something of our temporal being as historical agents. No other physical existent is historical in quite the same manner as a human being. Only a human self lives a present while being conscious of the past and future replete with memories, regrets, wishes and hope. *Time and Narrative* is a long reflection on how the meaning of human existence rests on how we understand the nature of our being in time and how time becomes "humanized" in the stories we tell one another.

The thesis of *Time and Narrative* shifts away from more traditional strategies in asking about the "what" of time to inquiring how our experience of time is embedded in the textuality of our existence. Such a strategy will not provide a speculative resolution to the inscrutability of time. Without suppressing either mortal time or cosmic time, it will preserve the paradox of time and pursue a "poetic" resolution to the aporetics of temporality (TN3 4).

Emplotment

In light of Aristotle's analysis of tragedy in his *Poetics*, Ricoeur will attempt to reveal how *poiesis* – the dynamic art of creating and composing plots – responds to the aporetic of time by organizing our ordinary experience of time into meaningful wholes. Time can be organized into wholes because we act and suffer in time. To the degree we understand how we plot our acting and suffering into stories we will understand how the ordinary experience of time, borne by daily acting and suffering, is refashioned by it passage through the grid of narrative.

In discussing tragedy, Aristotle says that the essence of *poiesis* is, on the one hand, the *mythos* or emplotment of the tragic poem, that is, the ability to plot events together into a system. On the other, the aim of the poem is the *mimesis* or the imitation – representation – of human action (*praxis*) (TN1 31ff.). Ricoeur emphasizes that *mimesis* is not a mere copying of reality. There is an active creative element in composing that goes beyond mere reproduction. *Mimesis* is not simply reduplication but a creative reconstruction (RI 134; HS 292). "Thanks to tragedy," for example, "we are prepared to look at human beings in a new way because human action is redescribed as greater, nobler, than actual life is" (RI 84). Like poetic figures in metaphor the configuration of a narrative suspends reference to the actual world in order to refigure it in a more meaningful manner.

Much of the first volume of *Time and Narrative* is devoted to a description of the formal aspects of narrative composition detailed as a three part mimetic process. Emplotment (*mimesis₂*), the most important, mediates between our pre-understanding of the world of practical action and events (*mimesis₁*) and the reception of the plot by a reader (mime*sis₃*) (TN1 53).

Emplotment would be impossible if we did not already possess an understanding of the language of "doing something" (TN1 57). This understanding of how action hangs together is referred to as *mimesis₁* (*prefiguration*). Each of us employs a "*semantics of action*" to readily distinguish "action" from mere physical movement and events (RI 433). A rich assortment of adverbs are embedded in language indicating in some way the temporal ordering of action: then, after, before, since, until, while, during, each time that, now that, and so forth. Further, long before we recount an event we have some precomprehension of how incidents and circumstances unfurl themselves without having to be repeatedly instructed as to what constitutes a beginning, an ending, an intervention and a tragic situation.

In terms of *mimesis₂* (*configuration*), or the actual emplotment, two points are vital. First, it is the activity that takes up a heterogeneous set of incidents, events and characters and transforms disparate entities into a story taken as a whole (TN1 65). It is the pivot between our actions and the story of our actions. This is not just the enumeration of events in a serial order but the organization of an intelligible whole that creatively links together such disparate factors as agents, ends, means, interactions, sudden reversals and violent effects. "To make up a plot is already to make the intelligible spring from the accidental, the universal from the singular, the necessary or the probable from the episodic" (TN1 41).

The plot is mediating in a second way by combining, in variable proportions, two temporal dimensions: the episodic dimension (chronological) and the configurational dimension (nonchronological). Owing to the episodic dimension events in narrative tend toward a linear representation of time in structuring the "then" and "and then" in order to answer the question "What next?" This permits us to follow a story "in the midst of contingencies and peripeteia under the guidance of an expectation that finds its fulfilment in the 'conclusion' of the story" (TN1 66). The configurational dimension, on the other hand, transforms the succession of events into one meaningful whole. Thanks to such a configurational arrangement the entire plot can be translated into one "thought" or "theme" from which can be gauged the beginning and the end allowing the story to be seen as a whole.

In short, the mimetic function of configuration, variously described by Ricoeur as the power of synthesis, "grasping together the heterogeneous" and schematizing, lies at the heart of emplotment. Under the auspices of the productive imagination it is the synthesizing work of emplotment that permits Ricoeur to consider narrative a form of semantic innovation along with metaphor.

Mimesis₃ (refiguration) completes the narrative arc. It is concerned with the relation between the text and the reader and is "the crucial moment of the entire analysis." While more will be stated later, it should be recalled that Ricoeur unequivocally rejects the static and closed conception of text. A text always points to an "outside." It projects a new world different from the one in which we live. What the reader interprets in the text is the proposing of a world that he or she may inhabit and project his or her ownmost powers. As such, composing a narrative resignifies the world in its temporal dimension to the extent that narrating, telling and reciting is "to remake action" following the work's invitation (TN1 81). In other words, human action as it is ordered by this or that emplotment refigures a previous configuration of the temporal features of the world.

Once the centrality of configuration has been established a large proportion of *Time and Narrative* is devoted to addressing one vital question: can the intentional aims of history and fiction be thought together in narrative as a poetic solution to the aporetic of time? Let us take history and fiction each in their own turn.

Historical Writing

Since the 1940s, there has been a general denigration of narrative in the field of historiography. Many positivist philosophers of history would suggest that there is little difference between causal explanation in the natural sciences and explanation in history (TN1 112). Some thinkers like Carl Hempel (1905-1997) contended that historical explanations are much like conclusions to arguments subject to general laws. Such nomological models see little cognitive value in the fact that histories tend to be written as narratives. Ricoeur is quick to remind us that historians too employ something of a narrative competence in organizing a diverse set of incidents and actions into wholes. At the heart of historical intention lies a form of "narrative understanding" that applies a type of logic able to plot causes, actions and goals into a coherent theme that can be read discursively (TN1 93; 159; 228). Such understanding does not operate as a function of strict chronology but utilizes what above was referred to as the episodic and configurational dimension of emplotment. The Hundred Year War and the French Revolution are rarely depicted in chronological detail alone as much as they are related and connected to other histories or plots that see diverse incidents and events grouped together in time in meaningful patterns.

Further, a historian emplots actions and events in order for them to be followed by a reader. To follow a historical account is the same as following a story in that we are pulled forward by "the sequence of actions and experiences done or undergone by certain number of people, real or imaginary" (TN1 150). Even when history deals with currents and trends it is the act of following the narrative that confers an organic unity on them. To be sure, history, while tied to narrative, is more than just story. There is the demand for evidence, argument and proof. "It is for this reason that historians are not simply narrators: they give reasons why they consider a particular factor rather than some other to be the sufficient cause of a given course of events" (TN1 186). But there is a deeper aspect to the role of narrative in history. Between historical narratives that claim to capture the "reality of the past" and the bias about the "unreality of fiction" there seems to be an unbridgeable dissymmetry between the two narrative modes. The commonsense approach would argue that only historians refer to something "real" because the "having-been" about which they write was observable to witnesses in the past. The trouble is that "having-been" is never observable, it is only memorable. For this reason Ricoeur prefers to speak about historical "traces" as "standing-for" and "taking the place of" such that any proposed historical *construction* of the past should be considered a *reconstruction*. If we are going to take seriously the historian's claim that historians describe "the past *as* it actually happened" then one cannot fail to note the metaphorical nature of the *as*. To say what things were *as* is to see them *as* – much in the same way a metaphor encourages "seeing as." It is more true, therefore, to say that historians do not describe the past as much as they redescribe it. In order to give shape to what can be known about the past, a historian makes something of a model or an icon of the past in order to represent it (TN3 152). Considering "there is no original given with which to compare the model" what really is at work is the imagination (TN3 153). Despite a historian's debt to the past and its victims, as well as his or her allegiance to historical traces of all sorts, a historian's narrative is still a creative imitation. "Here," Ricoeur suggests, "we reach the point where discovering and inventing are indistinguishable, the point … where the notion of reference no longer works, no more than does that of redescription. The point where, in order to signify something like a productive reference … we speak of productive imagination" (TN3 158).

Hence, what history borrows from fiction and literature is by no means limited to the level of composition or configuration. What often makes great historical works famous even though their reliability may have been eroded by documentary progress and advances in research is the tastefulness of their poetic art with respect to their way of "seeing the past." One and the same work can thus be a great book of history and a fine novel. What is surprising is that this interlacing of fiction and history in no way undercuts the project of "standing-for" belonging to history but instead helps to realize it (TN3 186).

Fiction

On the side of fiction Ricoeur mounts a similar critique with regard to the naïve concept of "unreality" applied to the projections of fiction. Like history fiction is about human action in that narratives represent (*mimesis*) what human beings do. But "it is only through reading that the literary work attains complete significance, which would be to fiction what standing-for is to history" (TN3 158). It must be recalled from the previous chapter concerning "the world of the text" that hermeneutics refuses to reduce a text to a closed system of immanent relations. The world of the text marks the opening of the text to its "outside." The very purpose of fiction's configuration of human action is to affect the reader in some way. Fictional narratives are not mere forms of entertainment using fantasy as a diversion. They make a difference in the world. Following Aristotle, Ricoeur argues that "catharsis sets the reader free for new evaluations of reality that will take shape in rereading" (TN3 176). Setting us free from the actual world, fiction aids in augmenting our perception of reality.

If reading were approached as "an aesthetic of reception" then one would see that the narrative and the reader are engaged in a synergetic relation (TN3 166ff). Where the story is our connection to the plot's capacity to model experience, it also becomes a potential "set of instructions" that the individual reader or the reading public executes in a passive or creative manner (TN1 77). "It is indeed through the anticipatory imagining of acting that I 'try out' different possible courses of action and that 'I play' ... with possible practices" (FT 177). As an aesthetic of reception reading becomes the place of "indeterminacy" where the text "depragmatizes" given experience. The text invites readers to wade through its excess of meaning thereby placing "readers in the position of finding a solution for which they themselves must find the appropriate questions, those that constitute the aesthetic and moral problem posed by the work" (TN3 173).

The dialectic between "the world of the text and the world of the reader" is at once an interruption in the course of action (to configure it by emplotment) and a new impetus to action (on behalf of the reader). This dialectic results directly from the confrontation of the imaginary world of the text and the world of the reader. To the extent that readers subordinate their expectations to those developed by the text they themselves become unreal to a degree comparable to the unreality of the fictive world. Reading then becomes a place, itself unreal, where reflection causes the reader to pause. In that pause it cannot be underestimated that "consciously or unconsciously" readers incorporate into their world the lessons of their reading. Reading, as such, is not a place where readers come to rest as much as it is a medium they pass through. What at one point was thought to be "unreal" has the potential to move us into the realm of "the real."

> This fragile union can be expressed in the following paradox: the more readers become unreal in their reading, the more profound and far-reaching will be the work's influence on social reality. Is it not the least figurative style of painting that has the greatest chance of changing our vision of the world? (TN3 179).

As reality becomes problematic under the shock of fiction each reader is invited to see the world from the horizon presented by the story. The world of the text and the world of the reader interpenetrate one another. Quoting Gadamer, Ricoeur argues for a "fusion of horizons" where the reader belongs to both the experiential horizon of the work imaginatively and the horizon of his or her action concretely (TN1 77). As the fiction suspends our belief in "the real," we find ourselves invited into a state of "non-engagement" where "we try new ideas, new values, new ways of being-in-the-world" (RI 128). In short, the imagination is given over to a free play of possibilities. Fiction is not just fanciful literature but possesses the power to shape the world of the reader. It offers a configuration of acting and suffering that can be applied to actual human acting and suffering.

> Fiction has the power to 'remake' reality and ... to remake real praxis to the extent that the text intentionally aims at a horizon of new reality that we may call a world. It is this world of the text which intervenes in the world of action in order to give it a new configuration or, as we might say, in order to transfigure it (FT 10).

Fiction's ability to redescribe reality is perhaps no more poignant than in its ability to refigure time. Ricoeur devotes the second volume of *Time and Narrative* to exploring how fiction plays imaginatively with the gap between cosmic time and mortal time. Fiction has the ability to reorient our sense of time since it is not subject to the constraints of documentary evidence. In looking at novels where the theme of time is accentuated such as Virgina Woolf's *Mrs. Dalloway*, Thomas Mann's *The Magic Mountain*, and Marcel Proust's *Remembrance of Things Past*, Ricoeur argues that these "tales about time" do not so much solve the central discontinuity of time as much as they sharpen it and make it productive. Such novels are the place where a truly human time is expressed in that they profoundly portray the dramatic conflict of living souls contending with a discordance that lies at the heart of human existence. Fiction opens up "an unlimited career to the manifestation of time" and provides us, the reader, with a fictive experience of time. A fictive experience of time is one that presents imaginative variations on the temporal aspects of being-in-the-world proposed by the text. It constitutes what Ricoeur calls "a transcendence immanent in the text" (TN2 101). In freeing themselves from the linear aspects of time novels, like those above, plunge the reader into a variety of temporal experiences "offering in each instance a different figure of recollection, of eternity in or out of time, and, ... of the secret relation between eternity and death" (TN2 101). Each configuration of human time emplotted in a narrative is a prelude to a forthcoming refiguration in light of the experiences of the reader. Again, the recalling of these experiences in fiction is not to solve the existential discordance between comic time and mortal time but to see how a poetic solution – through narrative – gives time a face, so to speak, and render temporal experience more meaningful.

Lastly, in the same way that history employs aspects of fiction to represent the past, fiction undergoes a certain "historization" in two senses. First, fiction deals with the "quasi-past" of actions "as if" they had taken place. Ricoeur sees events recounted in a fictional narrative as past facts for the narrative voice. As the narrative voice speaks, it recounts what *for it* has taken place. To enter into fiction is to enter into a pact where the reader believes that the events related by the narrative voice belong to the past of that voice (TN3 190). Second, while fiction is freed from the constraints placed by "the trace" on historical writing, it is nonetheless bound internally by the very thing it projects outside of itself. Every writer attempts to impart a vision and to articulate impressions of various depth and breadth. "Free from ..., artists must still make themselves free for ..." the faithful expression of their deepest impressions. If this were not the case then how could the anguish and suffering of artistic creation be explained – expressed as it is so vividly in, for example, the correspondence and diaries of a van Gogh and Cezanne. The stringent law of creation, which is to render as perfectly as possible the vision of the world that inspires the artist, corresponds, Ricoeur submits, feature by feature to the responsibility of the historian to render the past as truthfully as possible on behalf of its victims (TN3 177).

The Interweaving of History and Fiction – Historical Consciousness

The point of Ricoeur's long analysis has been to reveal the existence of a symmetry between fictional narrative and historical narrative based on the universal character of narrative configuration where, in both forms of narrative, the act of emplotment forges a "temporal synthesis of the heterogeneous." In the end, both forms of narrative, historical and fictive, humanize time. By writing history and telling stories we provide "shape" to the enigma of time. Ricoeur's analysis shows that history makes use of fiction and fiction has a historical component. So strong is the mutual borrowing that Ricoeur could with some confidence say that all history is fictionalized and all fiction is historicized. The result of this "interweaving" is what Ricoeur calls *the historical present* which he considers the proper present, the authentic present to humankind. None of us enters life without being implicated in the story of other people (family, community, culture, nation, or even a religious tradition). Each one of us belongs to an entanglement or "living imbrication" of stories (TN1 75). This entanglement is a "pre-history" that binds every other story to a larger whole that gives us a background and a tradition. The historical present is a hinge-point between accepting this background in a pre-critical manner and acquiring a historical consciousness where we realize the past is indeed not carved in stone but that each member of a community, each storyteller, has a stake in the past and the future.

The historical present, therefore, is neither the experience of a particular chronological moment nor a particular moment of inspiration and *kairos*. Such a present is not presence but the time of initiative, that is, the time when the weight of history that has already been made is deposited, suspended, and interrupted, and when the dream of history yet to be made is transposed into responsible decision (TN3 208). The verb "to begin" expresses the historical present better than all the substantive forms, including that of presence. "To begin" is to give a new course to things. It is the awareness that the world is not fully actualized and that now is the time *for me* to act. The historical present is the axial point where history both ends and begins; it is where initiative demands the making of history. It is the realization that the "established facts of history" are never irrevocably established. For Ricoeur, the future has priority over the past; the past in turn is never complete and always remains unfinished so that its real efficacy lies in its indetermination and reinterpretation. If a tradition is understood to

73

be the accumulation of stories that do not necessarily bestow upon us an invariant form of knowledge, then we must accept the hermeneutical challenge that what history does offers us is "a chain of interpretations and reinterpretations" (TN3 222). Our knowledge of the past is not one of "mastery over" but of always "being-affected." History is always "effective history" to the degree we realize that every expression of hope and expectation in the present re-opens the past. If our stories tell us about time, that time is undeniably historical. We are never finished being-affected-by-the-past. Living an "effective history" is thus a humbling experience. "The hermeneutical approach shifts the problematic from the sphere of knowledge into that of being-affected-by, that is, into the sphere of what we have not made" (TN3 228).

The historical present as the touchstone of a hermeneutics of historical consciousness is an attitude toward existence that does not merely imbibe a tradition unaware of all of its pretensions but seeks to reconcile humanity to it tasks and challenges. As stated above, it has been Ricoeur's contention all along that in refiguring action into narrative the text has the capacity to transform the world of the reader. Reading is not a mindless adoption. The situation of the reader will always exert its influence. In *Oneself an Another*, Ricoeur's next work, he will begin to talk about human agency. It is human agents, holding certain political and ethical beliefs, that are impelled to change institutions and practices – not texts. What is of ultimate importance is the element of personal initiative and intervention articulated through the power to listen, to speak, to read and to act. Nonetheless, it is the narrative mode, with its mimetic circle of prefiguration-configuration-refiguration *vis-à-vis* human action that permits a subtle analysis of those momentous but complicated steps by which human beings encounter and transform a tradition.

Narrative Identity

At the end of *Time and Narrative* an important theme arises from the interweaving of historical and fictive narrative. It is the notion of "narrative identity" that "crowns" the entire analysis (TN3 305, n. 8). Ricoeur sees narrative identity appearing in the midst of the dynamic dialectic he detailed between the signals provided by a narrative text and the act of reading. Let us briefly retrace these steps.

On the side of the author and the text is the role of emplotment. This is the way in which we arrange events and action that give a sense of wholeness to the story with a beginning and an end. Emplotment is what makes a story intelligible. Emplotment, under the aegis of what Ricoeur calls narrative intelligence or understanding, is the ability to take discordant events and heterogeneous episodes of human action and tie them together into a coherent plot permitting a concordant or tentative readability to our lives. It is what draws the manifold of events into one temporal whole. The construction of plots is the place where events become episodes and episodes become the stuff of stories.

When one asks such questions as "Who acts and suffers?" and "Who tells their story of tragedy, of joy?" a particular narrative category is recognized, namely, that of character. Each narrative is a recounting of someone being and doing – of undergoing and enduring. In answering the questions "Who endures?" and "Who undergoes?" Ricoeur's response is predicated on the assertion that someone performs actions. That someone is always a self, a characterized self that never stands over and against the exigency of acting and suffering. It is only in the telling our individual stories, over time, that a durable character becomes recognizable as belonging to a certain family, locality, tradition and culture. This character, in turn, finds him or herself enmeshed in a complex web of prior stories that make up a narrative heritage founded upon the epics, tragedies and dramas (both orthodox and subversive, both real and unreal) handed down to us by our culture.

On the other side of the dialectic, that of the reader, note has already been made that a text and a reader stand in a synergetic relation. A text sets up a novel space of indeterminacy for the reader where normal expectations are suspended and other variations on themes, dilemmas and crisis are presented. The text provides a world to be inhabited by the reader. It creates a distance from the everyday world of the reader by "depragmatizing" it. The work breaks open the narrowed and hard categories that define the world of the reader presenting possible levels of meaning not previously perceived.

Subsequently, the effect of emplotment does not end with the text but with the reader. The significance of a story finds its springboard of change in what the reader brings to it. The world of the text and the world of the reader interpenetrate one another as a "fusion of horizons." In this way a work is transfiguring in that it points us toward what is outside of us, toward the practical field of worldly encounters.

Invited by the zones of indetermination and layers of interpretations embodied in a text, each unity of awareness embodied by the reader, from the temporal to the ethical, becomes open for refiguration. "Refiguration" constitutes the "active re-organization of our being-in-the-world performed by the reader following the invitation of the text to become the reader of oneself" (PR 47). Emploting human action and reading are not pieces of a puzzle or fixed perches of rest but mediums that I, the reader pass through in search of an answer to the elusive question of "who am I?" The narrative function underpins what I can know about myself. It is the basis for "narrative identity."

Narrative identity is not established on the basis of an "indecomposable cogito" or an "impermeable unitive substance." It is not based on some permanently subsisting substance (*idem*) but on a living tissue of narrated stories that permits the recognition of a self (*ipse*) (TN3 246). Unlike an egological entity based on an immutable substance, self-constancy of the narrative self will include change and mutability within the cohesion of a lifetime. Where it is possible to compose several plots based on the same incident, it is just as possible to tell different – even opposed – plots about our lives. In recounting events, the historical aspect of narrative formation draws the plot toward a chronicled documentary fragment while the fictional aspect, with its penchant for imaginative variation, tends to destabilize narrative identity. In this sense narrative identity continues to make and unmake itself over the course of a lifetime (TN3 249).

To give narrative identity less of an abstract rendering, Ricoeur calls to mind the strong narrative component in "the working through" process well-known in psychoanalytical experience. The possibility of a cure resides in the hope of substituting a coherent and acceptable story for the fragments of memories and facts that are intelligible as well as unbearable. If we accept the premise that subjects recognize themselves in the stories they tell about themselves, then it is in psychoanalysis that we see how the story of one's life comes to be constituted through a series of rectifications – or refigurations – applied to previous narratives (TN3 247).

In the end the inception of narrative identity between mortal time and cosmic time does not lead to a mastery over the inner sense of temporal experience or to some stoic reconciliation with the cosmos. The inscrutability of time emerges victorious from the struggle. It cannot be the captive of any one plot no matter how tall the tale (TN3 261). Time's refiguration in narrative gives rise to the exigence to think more and to speak differently. While time will forever remain inscrutable it was Ricoeur's wish to show us how the time of narrative and narrative identity can collude to speak both to the threatening power of temporal passage and to an ungraspable eternity that seems mute before the burden of our cares.

Ricoeur's presentation of narrative identity in *Time and Narrative* is short and cursory. In subsequent papers he will universalize the role of narrative, making it fundamental to the emergence and reality of the self. "If it is true that fiction cannot be completed other than life, and that life can not be understood other than through stories we tell about it, then we are led to say that a life *examined*, in the sense borrowed from Socrates, is a life *narrated*" (RI 435). But what exactly is a narrated life? On the surface one might find the notion of narrative identity incredulous since life is lived and not told. Ricoeur's response to such questions is twofold.

First, the claim has already been made with regard to *mimesis₁* that we each possess a type of pre-narrative structure of experience that gives us the right to speak of "life as *an activity and a desire in search of a narrative*" (RI 434). Ricoeur believes that in the mixture of doing and undergoing of action that makes up the very texture of life there is a narrative intelligibility at work that seeks to imitate this mixture in a creative manner. Enveloped in a single glance life appears "as the field of a constructive activity, deriving from the narrative intelligence through which we attempt to recover (rather than impose from without) *the narrative identity which constitutes us*" (RI 436).

Second, life is no more than a biological phenomenon if it is not interpreted. Thanks to the narrative excess of order, coherence and unity, there is "always *more* order in what we narrate than in what we have actually already lived" (RI 468). Moreover, none of us enters into the communicative matrix of a community unconnected to the stories handed down to us by family and culture. We learn almost vicariously to apply to ourselves the concert of narrative voices that make up the symphony of great works, epics, tragedies, dramas and novels. Eventually, in light of this "concert of narrative voices," each of us becomes our own narrator without becoming authors and bearing the mask of a fictive *persona*.

> In this sense, it is certainly true that life is lived and the story told. An unbridgeable distinction remains, but it is, in part, abolished through our capacity to appropriate in the application to ourselves the intrigues we received from our culture, and our

capacity of thus experimenting with the various roles that the favorite *personae* assume in the stories we love best. And so we try to gain by means of *imaginative variation* of our *ego* a narrative understanding of ourselves, the only kind of understanding that escapes the pseudo-alternatives of pure change and absolute identity (RI 437).

Narrative, therefore, is no longer the reserved art of poets, dramatists and novelists. It is neither disguise nor decoration. Is it not true that we dream in narrative, daydream in narrative, remember, anticipate, hope, doubt, plan, gossip, hate, and love by narrative? Not only do we find ourselves embedded in a myriad of prior stories but also we are always fitting new daily events into our life narrative. We may not state this life narrative in a consistent autobiographical fashion, but ultimately the coherence of an individual life owes its unity to the mediation of the narrative function. In the end Ricoeur holds to three basic tenets concerning narrative identity: a) knowledge of the self is an interpretation; b) the interpretation of the self finds narrative, among other signs and symbols, to be a privileged mediation; c) this mediation borrows from history as much as from fiction making the life story a fictive history or a historical fiction comparable to biographies of great persons where fiction and history are blended to together.[7]

Ideology and Utopia

In his study of time and narrative Ricoeur never failed to underscore the vital importance of the imagination. Where Ricoeur began his philosophical anthropology with a phenomenological description of the will, the problems of the will were eclipsed by his hermeneutical turn toward language. This, in turn, led to the vital role of narrative with regard to human meaning, identity and creativity. "It is by an understanding of the worlds, actual and possible, opened by language that we may arrive at a better understanding of ourselves" (RI 490). The key to this "better understanding" lies in the creative act of reading. Reading, Ricoeur emphasizes, is more dependent on imagination than on the will. The referent of narration, namely human action, is never raw or immediate reality but finds itself always already in a nebula of meaning and tradition. Human creativity, especially in literature, is in some sense a response to this sedimentation of meaning and tradition. Not only literature but narratives of many sorts call daily existence into question and challenge our reading of both history and praxis. "Narrative is a redefining of what is already defined, a reinterpretation of what is already interpreted" (RI 469). Hermeneutics, as Ricoeur has come to understand it *vis-à-vis* philosophical anthropology, is not the discovery of some pristine immediacy but the demand to mediate again and again the "already interpreted" in a new and more creative fashion. "The mediating role of imagination is forever at work in lived reality" (RI 470). There is no lived reality – no human or social reality – which is not already represented in some sense. Every society possesses or is part of a *social imaginary*, that is, an ensemble of symbolic discourses (the literary, the scientific, and the political) that mediate human reality.

The topic of the social imaginary addresses an important question raised by Ricoeur's emphasis on narrative. It deals with the fact that narratives can project false worlds and evil visions of the world (e.g., social nationalism and racial discrimination). The notion that fictions can refigure or remake reality has not been an idea lost on political propagandists of all sorts. Every configuration of a social agenda, even ones with deep historical roots, have the potential to become "an official doctrine" and justify the power of the dominant class, the ruling party or tyrants. The question becomes a problem of reference. In a world so mediated by narrative how are we to judge the real from the imaginary?

Ricoeur attempts to overcome the dichotomy between the real and the imaginary by examining it under two limits, ideology and utopia. In *Lectures on Ideology and Utopia* (1986), he sees the social imaginary as representing the ensemble of mythic and symbolic discourses that serve to guide and motivate its citizens. This imaginary can function as a rupture or a reaffirmation (IU 265). As reaffirmation the imaginary operates as an "ideology" which repeats and represents the foundational symbols and discourse of a society thus preserving its identity. Every nation, for example, sets aside dates to commemorate the founding act which established it: the American Declaration of Independence, the French Revolution, the Soviet revolution, and so on (IU 261; HS 225). Even non-revolutionary nations and societies ceremoniously recall their originating myths and stories in hope of insuring some sense of ideo-logical continuity with regard to purpose and vision. Images and inter-pretations always intervene as the distance from the inaugural event increases. The danger with any ideology is that such reaffirmation can become perverted by monopolistic élites into a mystificatory discourse that serves to uncritically legitimate, or worse, glorify the established political powers. "In such instances, the symbols of a community become fixed and fetishized; they serve as lies" (RI 475).

On the other hand there exists the imaginary of rupture, a discourse of utopia that works in the opposite direction by introducing a sense of novelty, difference, and discontinuity with the past and present. Utopia means "nowhere" and it is from this extra-temporal nonplace that becomes the vantage point to take a fresh look at our reality. Utopian discourses pose the formidable challenge to "what-is" and perform the function of social subversion (FT 184). They are the mode in which we radically rethink the nature of family, consumption, government and religion by introducing imaginative variations on such topics (IU 16). As such, utopian images are critical of ideological power and challenge fossilized categories of tradition by pointing society towards an "elsewhere" and what is "not yet." Utopian discourses are not a solution in themselves. They too can be embraced in a dogmatic and orthodox manner and replace the ideological images they sought initially to dismantle and replace. Ricoeur reminds us, for example, of the Marxist-Leninist utopian call for the "withering away of the State" that failed to undertake the genuine measures to ever achieve such a goal. It ended by erecting no more than "a mere alibi for the consolidation of the repressive powers to be" (RI 475). Utopian dreams, regardless of their noblest hopes, can degenerate into mystificatory ideologies when dreamers, thinkers, and social reformers fail to follow through on the concrete practice that would bring such ideas into reality.

Ricoeur sees the two faces of the social imaginary – the ideological and the utopian – as essential to each other (FT 308ff). A society becomes stymied in its past or blinded by its misbegotten designs for its future when either parameter becomes too predominant. "In short, *ideology* as a symbolic confirmation of the past and *utopia* as a symbolic opening towards the future are complementary" (RI 475). Ideology as a system of hardened edicts, rules and paradigms established by past tradition is politically pathological if not directed toward some future goal or utopia. It is the social imaginary that holds the past and future in a creative tension so that experience and expectancy can have a fruitful dialogue. But such dialogue is not necessarily a readily coherent one and it is hardly a progressive dialectic with a foreseeable outcome. By nature, the tension between the two is insurmountable. Where the ideological imagination tends toward integration and repetition, the utopian tends to be "excentric." It is even often impossible to decide if a given mode of thought is ideological or utopian. "The line can only be drawn after the fact and on the basis of a criterion of success that, in its turn, can be questioned, inasmuch as it rests on the claim that only what has succeeded was just" (FT 186). In the absence of a standpoint of absolute knowledge to know what is best we must preserve a hermeneutical discourse between the two forms of social imagination, something akin to what has been averted into previous chapters concerning the conflict of interpretations. If we take Ricoeur's arguments seriously, that our sense of reality is always a mediated one based on language, texts and tradition, then there is no reason to assume there exists some nonideological layer of reality that will act as a foundation. As effective historical agents each of us is invited to participate in the social imaginary of culture – for better or for worse.

Let us conclude by returning to the remarks made at the opening of the chapter regarding metaphor, narrative function and semantic innovation where Ricoeur defended the claim that we shatter and increase our sense of reality as we shatter and increase language. We cannot separate the real from our interpretation of it. Our only access to the real depends on our metaphorical finesse to refigure it from a previous configuration. The ideology-utopia dialectic is the social dimension of this dynamic under the auspices of the social imaginary. We are always trying to escape the clutches of a false consciousness that would diminish language's creative and inventive qualities to show us what remains possible and thinkable. To give up this dialectic tension between ideology and utopia is to suppress the reaches of imagination and the potential of our humanity to think and to live differently.

Endnotes

1. Paul Ricoeur, "The Power of Speech: Science and Poetry," *Philosophy Today* 29 (1985): 59-70.
2. Ricoeur distinguishes between a live and dead metaphor. The former is an instantaneous creation, a semantic innovation which has no status in an already established language. A dead metaphor like "the leg of a chair" is a semantic innovation whose novelty has waned through repetition and become part of a speaking community's lexicon. Once a

term in a lexicon, a metaphor is no longer a metaphor but belongs to the polysemy of language. It becomes a fact of language and ceases to be act of discourse.

3. Paul Ricoeur, "The Power of Speech: Science and Poetry," 67.

4. *Ibid.* 68; see also RM 313.

5. Where *The Rule of Metaphor* spoke of metaphorical reference in terms of *redescription*, in *Time and Narrative* Ricoeur will prefer the term *refiguration*. This latter term deals much more with the way the reader sees the world mediated by texts where redescription tended to focus attention on the thing being redescribed and how new aspects of reality are brought to light.

6. Ricoeur's thesis in *Time and Narrative* can be stated in a manner akin to a hermeneutical circle. Narrative and temporality belong to a reciprocal relationship in that temporality is the structure of existence that reaches language in narrativity, and narrativity is the language structure that has time as its ultimate referent. See Paul Ricoeur, "Narrative Time," *Critical Inquiry* 7 (1980): 169-190 and "the circle of mimesis" TN1 71ff.

7. Paul Ricoeur, "Narrative Identity," *Philosophy Today* 35 (1991): 73-81).

5

The Self, the Other and Justice

The Primacy of Ethics over Morality

Three chapters of Ricoeur's next major work, *Oneself as Another* (1990), comprise what he summarily calls his "little ethics." Here, the themes of ethics, morality and practical wisdom are nested on top of a wider discussion of language, action, identity and narration. While this "little ethics" is his most sustained effort to elaborate an ethics within his hermeneutical inquiry, it would be erroneous to believe that the topic is only of late concern for Ricoeur. Numerous articles throughout his bibliography reveal that the relationship between ethics and politics has been an integral component of his philosophical anthropology.[1] The thematic thread that concretely links Ricoeur's ethical and political interests to his anthropology has been the question of human action, a concern that began with his *Philosophy of the Will*. His present incursion into ethics completes this theory of action.[2]

A Teleological Ethics

Oneself as Another is structured around the question of human action (OA 19). Chapters one to three treat the ways action can be *described* with specific reference to the Anglo-American theory of action. Chapters four to six discuss how actions can be told as a function of *narration*. Finally, Ricoeur opens his "little ethics" in chapters seven through nine by suggesting that human actions can be discussed in yet a third manner, namely, they can be *prescribed* and determined by the predicates "good" and "obligatory" (OA 169). In other words, actions have both an ethical and moral dimension. They can be evaluated under the aegis of various precepts.

Ricoeur distinguishes ethics from morality in seeing the former as "the *aim* of an accomplished life" and the latter as "the articulation of this aim in *norms* characterized at once by the claim to universality and by an effect of constraint." While references to Aristotle's teleological ethics and Kant's deontological heritage are obvious, Ricoeur will not follow either position in an orthodox manner. Instead, he proposes to defend three theses: a) the primacy of ethics over morality, b) the necessity of ethics to pass through the sieve of the norm, and c) the need to employ practical wisdom in singular cases (OA 170). As such, ethics is more fundamental than any norm. He defines the ethical intention teleologically as *"aiming at the 'good life' with and for others, in just institutions"* (OA 172). This condensed statement summarizes his "three-cornered ethics" that emphasizes the necessity to see the self, the other and institutions as intimately connected and necessary to answer the questions of how one is to act and the purpose of acting in a particular fashion.

By definition, a teleological position places the ultimate criterion of morality in some non-moral value such as happiness or welfare that results from the acts. This means that the ethical intention is animated by something prior to it and upon which it is dependent. In Ricoeur's terms, what animates the ethical intention is the wish for the good life. The aim for "the 'good life' with and for others, in just institutions" is an object of desire that includes the goods of justice and equitability. This desire – this hope for the good life – is the over-arching horizon that informs our actions in the present. Solitary individuals alone however cannot fulfill this desire. As Ricoeur states, "it is within the *interesse* that the hope (*le souhait*) of living well achieves its goal. It is as citizens that we become human. The hope to live within just institutions means nothing else" (TJ xv). The individual's desire to live well is always integrated with society's desire to live well.

In short, human actions are more than mere physical events. An agent initiates his or her actions with a particular goal in mind; they are instrumental or a means to an end. They are teleologically oriented. To ensure aims do not cultivate harm and injustice, actions are always subject to deontological considerations. While moral obligations must accompany our search along the interminable path toward "the good life," the ethical aim remains primary.

The Interminability of the Ethical Aim

Although Ricoeur makes no mystery of borrowing the notion of the "good life" from Aristotle, he has a different signification in mind. For Aristotle, the "good life" was achieved to the extent that one possessed the respected position, the sufficient wealth, the necessary virtue, the friends and the contemplative aptitude to do so. These finite goods were embedded in a Hellenic social order that was accepted as the best of all possible social orders in which free citizens could achieve their proper ends. In Ricoeur's appropriation of Aristotle the "good life" lacks the fixity and finiteness it had for the Stagirite. In *Oneself as Another*, Ricoeur readily agrees that "the fundamental basis for the aim of the 'good life' [is] in praxis" (OA 172), but that the content of the good life is "... the nebulous of ideals and dreams of achievements with regard to which a life is held to be more or less fulfilled or unfulfilled" (OA 179).

As such, the "good life" is not satisfied by the lived achievement of conditions within a finite social order alone. The "good life" is a notion that acts as a "horizon" or a "limiting idea" that permits us to gauge "... the search for adequation between what seems to us to be best with regard to our life as a whole and the preferential choices that govern our practices" (OA 179). The good life lies beyond our concept of it. It is not reducible to a set of particular ideals or material goals. As a limiting idea it acts as an interpretative key so that "... between our aim of a 'good life' and our particular choices a sort of hermeneutical circle is traced by virtue of the back and forth motion between the idea of the 'good life' and the most important decisions of our existence (career, loves, leisure, etc.)" (OA 179). In using the analogy of how part of a text is understood in relation to the whole and vice versa, the good life is always more than the sum of individual exercises of practical judgement. As a whole, the "good life" transcends the particular ends to which particular practices aim but nonetheless orders them. It is in this sense that such an aim or *telos* as the "good life" is interminable.

The Centrality of Praxis

In referring to the opening lines of Aristotle's *Nicomachean Ethics*, Ricoeur reminds us that it was Aristotle who first taught us to seek the fundamental basis for the aim of the "good life" in action or, more technically, *praxis* (OA 172). He goes on to state that the second important instruction from Aristotle was the necessity to seek the structuring principle for the aim of the good life in "the teleology internal to praxis" (OA 172-3). What this means can be explicated with regard to several levels of praxis peculiar to human beings.

Excluding mere gestures, Ricoeur sees human beings involved in a hierarchy of practices. On one level, human beings engage in jobs, skills, arts and games that are co-operative activities whose constitutive rules are socially established. These practices are learned from someone and the training relies on a tradition. Our success or virtuosity at such practices requires the recognition by other practitioners such that, with or without an organized framework, our practices are open to comparisons in terms of "standards of excellence." These standards act at one point as a form of self-appraisal and, at another, a potential norm. In this sense, a practice has a set of "internal goods" or ends immanent to it. This is the teleology internal to the practice itself. Second, beyond the practices mentioned above, there is another level of praxis more properly understood as "life plans" that include vocational life, family life, the life of leisure and so on. While a life plan might single out a particular goal we never stop rectifying our initial choices "moving back and forth between far-off ideals" (OA 177). Between practices and life plans there is a nesting of finalities, one inside the other.

At a third level of praxis someone is the author of his or her action to the extent that he or she interprets himself or herself in terms of the skills and arts in which one is engaged. This interpretation is undertaken in accordance with the competence and the degrees of excellence determined by rules that regulate the practice. It is here for the first time that we see that the gap between action and morality narrow since the interpretation of action is open to disputes over such judgements of excellence. There is a fourth level of praxis already addressed above, namely, the good life. It is the "good life" that is more evaluative than descriptive. It closes the gap between just action and morality in that it becomes the horizon, or as above, "the nebulous of ideals and dreams" from which we evaluate the intermediary series of rules, standards, goods, plans and self-interpretation that we pass through over the course of a lifetime. More poignantly, "the 'good life' is 'that in view of which' all these actions are directed, actions which were nevertheless said to have their ends in themselves" (OA 179). Hence, an act is never just an act. An act is always nested in a hierarchy of finalities where the "good life" maintains a tension between the closed and the open within the global structure of praxis. It is "a higher finality" internal to human praxis.

Moral Agency and the Other

Given all the references to action the obvious question becomes "who acts?" The actual power-to-act in the self, the "I can," is referred to as a "primitive datum" with its temporal locus situated in the lived body (OA 111). The lived body is my body that has a double allegiance to the order of physical bodies and to that of persons. The lived body lies at the point of articulation between my own power to act and the things that belong to the world order. The notion of lived body acts as the intermediary between action and agent and serves as a "propaedeutic to the question of selfhood" thereby permitting a response to the "who" of imputable acts and responsibility (OA 113).

The presentation of moral agency in *Oneself as Another* is couched in a larger discussion that moves toward a hermeneutics of the self or selfhood. It is continuous with the previous study of narrative identity detailed in the last chapter. The aim in the present work is to identify the subject of action with the subject of imputation under the rubric of "selfhood," that is, a moral agent who responds to "the nakedness of the question ... 'Who?' ... with the proud answer 'Here I am!'" (OA 167). In elaborating the subject of action as it is described, narrated and prescribed, Ricoeur will delineate the multiple points of reference to a power of agency. The ethico-moral identity that Ricoeur works toward is characterized primarily by the "*power-to-do*" thereby making the agent responsible for his or her initiatives and interventions "in the course of the world, ... intervention[s] which effectively causes changes in the world" (OA 109). Delineating this power-to-do is only prefatory to understanding "*power-in-common* ... of the members of a historical community to exercise in an indivisible manner their desire to live together" (OA 220). In the tenth chapter, Ricoeur will attempt to secure an ontology for these multiple uses of the term "acting" by suggesting we take Aristotle's notion of being as akin more to "the metacategory of being as act and as power" than as a theory of substance (*ousia; substantia*) (OA 305ff).

Ricoeur locates his hermeneutics of the self beyond what he calls the modern exalted *cogito* of Descartes and the dispersed and shattered *cogito* spoken of by Nietzsche. It begins with a recognition of a certain polysemy regarding the question who? (who speaks? who acts? who tells his or her story? who is responsible?). The retrieval of the "who" questions prevents an obfuscation between event and action and reminds us that actions are open for evaluation and occur as the

87

initiative of a particular agent.

At the heart of the problem of selfhood and personal identity is the issue of temporality. "The person of whom we are speaking and the agent on whom the action depends have a history, are their own history" (OA 113). More precisely it is a question of what Ricoeur calls *idem*-identity or the problem of *sameness* over time. Normally we employ such parameters as numerical identity, qualitative identity and some form of material indicator of permanence in time (e.g. finger prints, dental records, genetic structure) in order to assert the sameness of identity over time. Such material indicators are vital when determining, for example, the identity of an alleged criminal long after the actual crime has been committed. Ideally there would be little problem if an unequivocal substratum to our identities existed. But this reduces the question of identity to "what" and not "who." Ricoeur is adamant in wanting to show that identifiable agents or selves exist behind actions, not substratums of sameness! The central question is whether or not "there [is] a form of permanence in time that is a reply to the question 'Who am I?'" (OA 118).

In response, Ricoeur makes a distinction between identity as spatiotemporal selfsameness (*idem* – sameness) and the capacity of an agent to initiate an imputable action (*ipse* – selfhood). To *idem*-identity corresponds the model of character. We have already come across the term "character" twice with reference to Ricoeur's early works. In *Freedom and Nature*, character was one of the absolutely permanent and involuntary aspects of human experience to which we can only consent. In *Fallible Man,* at the level of practical analysis, character dealt with limited perspective, the finite pole of a mediation under the aegis of respect toward the infiniteness of happiness. In *Oneself as Another*, character represents the stable pole of sameness. It designates the set of permanent dispositions that have undergone innovation and sedimentation in the acquisition of habits that yield the constancy of what permits us to recognize that person as particularly that person. It answers the "what" of the "who" (OA 122).

The other model of permanence in time, *ipse*-identity, is represented by keeping one's word. Unlike character this model lies solely in the dimension of "who?" Where the continuity and perseverance of character are one thing, the constancy of friendship and the perseverance of faithfulness are quite another. Keeping one's word is a challenge to time and to a denial of changes to mood and feelings under the self-imposed rubric of "I will hold firm" and "I am accountable for my actions to another." Here, the "who I am" is maintained regardless of change yet depends least of all on the parameters of sameness found in character (OA 124). The promise of one's word is a fidelity to self anchored in the presence of the other and not reducible to a form of *idem*-identity.

While on the surface both *idem*-identity and *ipse*-identity seem irreconcilable, Ricoeur will argue that both *together* express more precisely the two faces of a person's temporal identity. In refusing to hypostasize either sense of identity Ricoeur suggests we seek their dynamic mediation in a category that seems ready-made to fit their aporetic nature, namely narrative identity. Narrative identity submits the poles of sameness and selfhood to the imaginative variations of the text. By varying the relation between them the two meanings of permanence in time are made evident. In everyday experience these meanings tend to overlap and merge with one another (OA 148). The narrative function is vital here because it doesn't provide a speculative response to the aporias of identity but makes "them productive on another order of language." It becomes "the *poetic reply*" to the paradox of personal identity (OA 147).

Narrative is vital in yet another way. In *Time and Narrative*, Ricoeur argued that the self does not know itself immediately, but only indirectly, through the detour of narration and hence, as an interpretation. We have already crossed the path of interpretation and the self above in speaking about the centrality of praxis. There we said that someone is the author of his or her action to the extent that he or she interprets himself or herself in terms of skills, arts, games and so forth. On the ethical plane this self-interpretation, or self-evaluation of behavior, appears as self-esteem (OA 180). This is because our practices, whether they be hobbies, professions or sports are measured by standards of excellence. In esteeming the excellence or success of our actions we begin to appreciate ourselves as the author of our own actions. We begin to appreciate our capacity to act in terms of the "I can" mentioned above. The important twist is that being-able-to-do on the practical plane corresponds on the ethical plane to being-able-to-judge. As author of our actions we will evaluate them by imputing them with either esteem or regret. Consequently our very sense of self and our actions involves us in an

> ... unending work of interpretation applied to action and to oneself [where] we pursue the search for adequation between what seems to us to be best with regard to our life as a whole and the preferential choices that govern our practices. ... By the same token, our concept of the self is greatly enriched by this

89

relationship between interpretation of the text of action and self-interpretation. On the ethical plane, self-interpretation becomes self-esteem. In return, self-esteem follows the fate of interpretation. Like the latter, it provokes controversy, dispute, rivalry – in short, the conflict of interpretations – in the exercises of practical judgement (OA 179).

The reader must not lose sight of the purpose behind this "unending work of interpretation." At one level the unity of these interpretations *is* the narrative unity of life as we learned in the previous chapter. Owing to it we have an identity and a history to situate ourselves. At another level, perpetual interpretation has a further end, namely, the "good life." Not only are we self-interpreting beings but self-correcting ones as well. Allegiance to interpretation raises the self and its aims above deterministic arguments. It is the key to recovering the "more primitive and more radical foundation to moral philosophy," namely, "the joyous affirmation ... of the effort to be ... at the origin of ethics' very dynamic." In light of the "good life" it is interpretation that guarantees

> this movement (*parcours*) of actualization, this odyssey of freedom across the world of works, this proof-testing of the being-able-to-do-something (*pouvoir-faire*) in effective actions which bear witness to it. Ethics is this movement between naked and blind belief in a primordial 'I can,' and the real history where I attest to this 'I can.'[3]

The aim of the good life on behalf of the self is however only the first component of Ricoeur's "three-cornered ethics." There is also the need to live with others and the need to abide in just institutions. Turning to this second component, Ricoeur argues that our need of the other is so radical that self-esteem is coeval with solicitude for the other; that is, solicitude is not merely altruistic, it is necessary. This means that our very realization of our capacity to act, to initiate, to intend, and to project requires the mediation of the other. This brings us back to Ricoeur's claim that the ethical aim must pass through the sieve of the norm – that there is a place for duty and obligations. It is the place where ethics must give way to morality since the aim of the good life invariably runs up against violence in all of its forms. Where self-esteem and esteem for others belong to the ethical aim, respect of self and others belong to the level of morality.

Morality encompasses a wide spectrum that ranges from the injunction coming from outside oneself ("Thou shalt not ...") to sympathy for the other that comes from the self. This wide spectrum finds its median point in friendship. While a variety of relations exist in friendship, the type Ricoeur has in mind is one that is rich in mutual esteem where each party desires what is best for the other. Such a desire issues from the shared admission of each other's fragility and mortality. "To self-esteem, understood as a reflexive moment of the wish for the "good life," solicitude adds essentially the dimension of *lack*, the fact that we *need* friends; as a reaction to the effect of solicitude on self-esteem, the self perceives itself as another among others" (OA 192). Friendship however is not merely instrumental. While the mutuality of friendship may be reversible the persons who play these roles are not substitutable. The non-replace-ability and non-substitutability in friendship leads to a level of recognition that grounds our ethical feelings. Ricoeur calls it similitude. It signifies that I can acknowledge the other as a self like myself who is the author of his or her actions, preferences and solicitudes such that there is the mutual understanding of "you too ... as myself." It is the recognition of the shortest distance between the "I" and "you" where the esteem of the *other as oneself* and the esteem of *"oneself as an other"* are seen as equivalent (OA 194).

Justice

It is this undeniable need of the other that points the way toward justice, the last component of Ricoeur's "three-cornered ethics." Where friendships might unite small groups of people and achieve some modicum of equality, justice, by contrast, calls for the role of institutions since "the desire to live well" does not reach the end of its trajectory in solitude or friendship but in the setting of the city. Justice is integral to the wish to live well. This wish arises from the same source as does the desire – at the anthropological level – to seek the good and happiness. While we pride ourselves on being autonomous beings we would remain only shadows of our potential without institutional mediation and without a society that acknowledges such a value. To this end, the individual is indebted to institutions with the interest that they remain just institutions. Our role as moral agents is at once a role of citizenship. This role is not conditional or optional. Owing to the necessity of institutional mediation the goal of citizenship is the pursuance of just institutions – especially political institutions.

...the citizens who issue from this institutional mediation can only wish that every human being should, like them, enjoy such political mediation, which when added to the necessary conditions from a philosophical anthropology becomes a sufficient condition for the transition from the capable human being to the real citizen (TJ 10).

In *Oneself as Another*, Ricoeur situates the place of justice at the intersection of two axes (OA, studies 7-9; TJ xiiff). Upon the first axis, the horizontal, rest the various relations that comprise the dialogical constitution of the self. These consist not only of the fundamental I-thou relation that animates this dialogical constitution, but, as well, the entire network of interpersonal relations up to and including those mediated by institutions. Where the "other" for friendship is the "you," the "other" in the task of justice is "anyone" reflected in the adage "to each his own." On the second axis, the vertical, rest the levels of predicates indicative of moral evaluation such as the "good," the "legal" and the "equitable." The purpose of these orthogonal axes is to show that "the just" normally has two sides in its application to persons, their actions and institutions. On the teleological plane the just is an aspect of the good relative to the other with whom we hope to live well. On the deontological plane of obligation the just is identical with the legal.

Justice has a third element. It concerns difficult singular situations where practical wisdom must be exercised. In such situations the just is neither the good or the legal but the equitable. "The equitable is the figure that clothes the ideas in the incertitude and of conflict, or, to put it in a better way, in the ordinary – or extraordinary – realm of the tragic dimension of action" (TJ xxiv). We shall return to the tragic dimension of action shortly.

The topic of distribution is key to Ricoeur's discussion of justice and the role of institutions. It is key because it reveals the "mutation the sense of justice undergoes in passing from the teleological to the deontological point of view" (TJ xviii). "By 'institution'" Ricoeur means "the structure of *living together* as this belongs to a historical community – people, nation, region, and so forth – a structure irreducible to interpersonal relations and yet bound up with these in ... the notion of distribution" (OA 194). The introduction of the concept of distribution assures the transition from the interpersonal to the societal. While a society is always more than the sum of its members and the role each plays, it depends nonetheless on the participation of individuals. The concept of distribution is tied to that of justice in that it is institutions which govern the apportionment of roles, tasks, and advantages and disadvantages between members of a society. What is apportioned is what is materially valued and often scarce. It is the cooperative task of how "shares" are distributed to individuals – and thereby make each of us part of the whole – that demands just distribution and legitimate institutions. Distributive justice is about equality and its nature. "Equality is the ethical mainspring of justice" (OA 228).

Defining and standardizing equality however is not a simple task. While Aristotle may have made strong theoretical claims for preferring proportional equality to arithmetic equality, the former is not without serious problems concerning the just dispensation of goods, merit and wealth. The problem in adequately defining the notion of equality is a fundamental ambiguity that arises in pursuing the sense of justice in the idea of a just share. Should the accent be placed on the separation between what belongs to one person to the exclusion of the other, or, on the tie of cooperation and the community of interests established by the division? (OA 227ff). The tendency in the late 20th century, Ricoeur argues, has been to follow the former accent, in accentuating separation and the mutual disinterest in the interest of others. The result is a drift toward individualism and the desire to prescribe a method of just distribution by means of a strictly procedural conception of justice (deontological) that diminishes the need to incorporate particular ethical aims and convictions.

Practical Wisdom

The last thesis of Ricoeur's ethical reflections is the acknowledgement that even if ethical aims could be integrated theoretically with norms, a sense of justice, and distributive justice in particular, remains problematic. In terms of the latter he states that "no system of distribution is universally valid; all known systems express revocable, chance choices, bound up with the struggles that mark the violent history of societies" (OA 284). It is Ricoeur's point however not to leave decisions up to "chance choices" but to fetter out the best decision given all the arguments. The real test of the "best decision" is the appearance of particular cases that demand more than the application of a general norm (CC 92). The application of norms to situations is already the case in juridical procedures were a *corpus* of relatively homogenous laws exist and that have not been called into question. Ricoeur puts great value therefore in uncovering the vital dynamic in situations of decision where it is the very reference to the law that causes the problem. A classic example is the confrontation between Creon and Antigone in Sophocles' play *Antigone* (OA 241ff). In the course of the play both parties defend respectable spiritual values but in a particular dilemma these values become incompatible and the conflict eventually ends in the deaths of the antagonists. With this in mind Ricoeur devotes the last chapter of his "small ethics" to what he calls practical wisdom (*phronesis*) (OA 174-5; 249ff; TJ 154).

Practical wisdom is the discernment of action in particularly difficult cases that run the threat of being decided by a naïve moral situationism. It is evoked in what Ricoeur called above "the tragedy of action" which recognizes the fact that not all universal norms can be satisfied even if they are genuine moral norms. There are times when solicitude for the other – in cases of the law, medicine and everyday life – cannot be captured in the obedience to a universal norm. It is also the case that rules claiming universal moral validity clash with positive values that belong to particular historical and communal interests. Moreover, "the tragic evokes a situation where a human awakens painfully to the consciousness of a destiny or fatality which weighs in his or her life, nature, and very condition."[4] This tragic dimension of action calls for a clarification of conviction beyond convention and the impartiality of an abstract ethics.

Ricoeur discusses practical wisdom within two domains – the political and the interpersonal. At the political level, civic individuals are assumed to have the power to act and to be the author of his or her own actions. Such a power is tempered by the power-in-common in order for civic members of a community to live together well. Unfortunately this latter power is often corrupted by the will of domination that seems to be a constant reality of political life. The gap between power and domination erupts in what Ricoeur calls "the political paradox" – the fact that democracy is continually attempting to place domination under the control of the power-in-common which often results in yet another form of domination (OA 257). Consequently, the terms of "good" government with respect to "security," "prosperity," "liberty," "equality," "solidarity" and so forth remain fundamentally contentious and undecidable. No appeal to a universal norm would satisfy the need to explicate the plurality of sense latent in each of these terms. The result is that "the irreducible plurality of the ends of 'good' government implies that the historical realization of one set of values can be obtained only at the expense of another set; in short, this implies that one cannot serve all values at once" (OA

259). This makes politics as an institutional enterprise an inherently fragile enterprise. The need to constantly bridge the gap between power and domination, and to interrogate their terms of reference, moves the discussion from the conflicts within the rule of justice to the broader conflicts posed by the sense of justice, that is, *the need to move from moral norms per se to the ethical aim of the norms.*

The tragedy of action arises with even more poignancy in the domain of interpersonal life where respect for the law (universal norms) clashes with the respect for actual individual persons. For example, is it always the case that an individual should keep his or her promises as a condition of coherency to him or herself and the moral norm of promising keeping? Should someone keep his or her word with such rigidity in a particular circumstance as to violate a more intimate fidelity grounded in solicitude for the other? Human life invariably runs up against situations where respect for the law conflicts with respect for persons. The point is whether or not there is a type of Marcellian *disponibilité* or creative availability and openness to the other that is beyond the demands of legislated and historical norms (OA 268). Practical wisdom demands the arduous task of "inventing just behavior suited to the singular nature of the case," a just behavior that treads the delicate balance between suffering and happiness (OA 269).

This task of balance must be mediated by what Ricoeur calls critical solicitude, that is, solicitude that is guided by the care owing to each person in his or her uniqueness. This uniqueness becomes strikingly poignant in two particular situations: one dealing with the set of issues surrounding "the end of life," where it is necessary to decide whether or not to tell someone of their imminent death; and, second, the question of "the beginning of life," with regard to the "progressive appreciation of the rights of the embryo, then of the fetus" (OA 270ff). There are three features that guide practical wisdom in such situations. First, that the principle of respect and solicitude remains central, especially in cases where there is an intermediary zone of identity between biological beings and morally developed persons. Second, that there be an earnest search for the Aristotelian "just mean." This would be more than a cowardly compromise and include the task of reconciling opposing claims that would itself be above such claims. Third, to guard against arbitrary decisions, it is necessary to seek the counsel of the most competent and wisest advisors possible. "The *phronimos* [person of wise judgement] is not necessarily one individual alone" (OA 273). In requesting the counsel of others the call to debate and conflict is unavoidable.

Because debate and disagreement are unavoidable Ricoeur develops a subtle dialectic between argumentation and conviction, "which has no theoretical outcome but only the practical outcome of the arbitration of moral judgement in situation" (OA 287). What does he mean exactly by these two terms, "argumentation and conviction?" First, by argumentation, Ricoeur implies its dialectical relationship with interpretation. In the case of a legal process, for example, facts are problematic in both their description and evaluation. Facts are never just brute facts but charged with meaning and hence must be interpreted. In arguing the facts there is actually an interweaving of argumentation and interpretation that echoes Ricoeur's aphoristic formula "to explain more in order to understand better" (TJ 125-6). Furthermore, every interpretative process for Ricoeur has a creative function where imagination plays a role. The need to weigh resemblances and differences between precedent and similar cases is part of the argumentative process that leads to the construction of a novel decision for each situation. For Ricoeur, "whether one argues for or against assumes that one tries out in imagination the hypothesis of resemblance or difference" (TJ 125-6).

And what of convictions? Practical wisdom, in deciding on a course of action, arises as convictions are subjected to argumentation and bring the convictions that inform a possible decision into sharp relief. Central to Ricoeur's formulation is the belief that argumentation acts as a critical agency operating at the heart of convictions not to eliminate them but to bring them to the level of "well-considered convictions" (OA 288 modified translation).

In particular situations, it is these well-considered convictions that become the basis for concrete conduct. Such convictions however do not carry the weight of law or norms since they are called up precisely because of the inapplicability of universal norms to satisfy the demands of solicitude. In drawing upon our deepest wishes for the good life, well-considered convictions become our recourse to the primal resources of ethics which have not yet passed through the norm (OA 352). On the other hand, convictions are not something arbitrary: "the moment of conviction is not a substitute for the test of the rule; it arises at the end of a conflict, which is the conflict of duties" (OA 352). While on the surface this "conflict of duties" leads eventually to "the apparent better thing to do in the circumstance" (TJ 155), the dynamic of the conflict resides in what Ricoeur calls the "the reflective equilibrium between the ethics of argumentation and well-considered convictions" (OA 289 modified translation). This equilibrium arises from the fragile tension between the demands of teleology and deontology.

But there is more to say about well-considered convictions. It is in the last instance, when convictions become the basis for action, that they become indiscernible from "conscience." Conscience, or the heart of hearts as Ricoeur likes to call it, is still something more than conviction per se. Conscience is "attestation," that is, a confident belief and trust which attaches itself to the affirmation of the self as an acting and suffering being.[5] "The heart of hearts appears as the intimate assurance that, in particular circumstance, doubts, hesitations, inauthentic suspicions, hypocrisy, self-complacency and self-deception are swept away, and authorizes the acting and suffering person to say: Here I stand."[6]

This sense of resoluteness for Ricoeur is at once an openness and a call. In times of singular and difficult situations the moral subject operates not from an external imperative or commandment but as a response to an injunction voiced in the optative mood where "listening to the voice of conscience would signify being-enjoined by the Other" (OA 351). It is the peculiarity of finding oneself called upon in the second person (You there!) that rebounds in the conscientious recognition of "oneself as being enjoined to live well with and for others in just institutions and to esteem oneself as the bearer of this wish" (OA 352). Does conscience, in its plainest terms, merely signify the voice of the Other in the sense of others? Otherness for Ricoeur is "*being enjoined as the structure of selfhood*" (OA 354). It is a profound unity of *self-attestation* and of the *injunction* coming from the other. In this way none of us has mastery over the inner intimate certitude of existing as a self. Such certainty comes to us like a gift or a grace and not at our self-willed disposal.[7] The self is not the product of a strict auto-affection. The origin of this evocative voice of otherness, the voice that calls us not only to be a self but an ethical self, remains unbridged in Ricoeur's philosophical work.

The individual voice of conscience however is not the final arbiter of a moral decision. The decision taken at the end of a debate with oneself, in our heart of hearts, will be all the more worthy of being called wise if it issues from a council. "Wisdom in judging and the pronouncement of the wise judgement must always involve more than one person" (TJ 155). Ricoeur never tires in his insistence on this need for a plurality of voices regardless of the precarious nature of such a debate (OA 290). It is a reminder that our own autonomy is tied to others and that our own narrative is never our own entirely. Owing to our all too human need for institutions, few of us can refuse participation in the conflictual consensus that aim to keep our institutions just and able to arbitrate well the rival claims of our convictions that point us toward the good life.

Lastly, the term "fragility" that Ricoeur uses to describe the tension between teleology and deontology, between argumentation and interpretation, and between the various forms of distributive justice and well-considered convictions is not a capricious one on his part. It reflects not only the human weaknesses of misunderstanding because of semantic confusion and differences in basic convictions but recalls once again the description in *Fallible Man* of the fundamental disproportion that is human being. As human beings our very nature is to mediate between two modalities that belong to the totality of human being – the finite and infinite. This fundamental characteristic to mediate indicates our basic vulnerability as well as our strength. It means that many of our successes philosophically, socially, economically and politically will be tinged with "the pathétique of 'misery'" and indeed be fragile by the very fact that it is us – the fragile beings that we are -- who have taken as our task their construction and application. Yet, it is this same fragility that awakens each of us to the other who not only declares me responsible but who is also the very medium of my own identity. If we are going to take this fragility seriously and incorporate it into the field of public praxis, then the role of justice becomes more than a pragmatic and legal task. Justice and the institutions that dispense it become our necessary mediums of love. In this light, the formulation of all our codes – from penal codes to codes of social justice – must be supplemented, even tenaciously given the indefiniteness of the task, by generosity and compassion.[8]

Endnotes

1. See Paul Ricoeur, *Political and Social Essays,* eds. David Stewart and Joseph Bien (Athens, Ohio: Ohio University Press, 1974) and Part 3 of FT. An important summary is supplied in Bernard Dauenhauer, *Paul Ricoeur: The Promise and Risk of Politics* (Boston: Rowman & Littlefield Publishers, Inc., 1998).
2. Paul E. Reagan, *Paul Ricoeur: His Life and His Work,* 119.
3. Paul Ricoeur, "The Problem of the Foundation of Moral Philosophy," in *The Foundation and Application of Moral Philosophy:*

Ricoeur's Ethical Order, ed. H. J. Opdebeeck (Leuven: Peeters, 2000), 13-4.

4. Paul Ricoeur, "Fragility and Responsibility," in *Paul Ricoeur: The Hermeneutics of Action,* ed. Richard Kearney (London: Sage Publications, 1996), 15.

5. "Attestation" is a confidence in the self, an unsubstantiated confidence, that the self actually is and that the self can act. Attestation is a belief – an epistemic truth – that the self exists and that everyone exists as a self. In spite of suspicion, it is the assurance of being oneself acting and suffering. See the pertinent passages in OA 21-22; 299ff.

6. Paul Ricoeur, "From Metaphysics to Moral Philosophy," *Philosophy Today* 40, no. 4 (1996): 443-458.

7. *Ibid.* 455.

8. Paul Ricoeur, "Love and Justice," in *Paul Ricoeur: The Hermeneutics of Action,* 37.